WORLD Languages PROJECT

Sol Garson
Ruth Heilbronn
Barbara Hill
Cathy Pomphrey
Anna Valentine
Jenny Willis

HODDER AND STOUGHTON
LONDON SYDNEY AUCKLAND TORONTO

Copyright © 1989 Sol Garson, Ruth Heilbronn, Barbara Hill,
Cathy Pomphrey, Anna Valentine, Jenny Willis.

First published in Great Britain 1989

British Cataloguing in Publication Data

World languages project
  1. Languages. For schools
  I. Garson, Sol
  400
ISBN 0 340 41138 4

Typeset by Taurus Graphics, Abingdon.
Printed and bound in Great Britain for the educational publishing
division of Hodder and Stoughton, PO Box 702, Mill Road,
Dunton Green, Sevenoaks, Kent by St Edmundsbury Press Ltd,
Bury St Edmunds.

INTRODUCTION

This book is about languages, the languages of the world. In it you will learn about language families, the history of many languages and about the people who speak these languages. You will come across scripts written from right to left, learn how to read them and investigate the history of printing. You will hear different sounds, accents and intonations and tune your ear to many dialects and languages. You will encounter strange facts and information which will link your study of language to other subjects.

By studying the structure of other languages, you will become more familiar with your native tongue and more interested in the grammar of languages, especially when you invent your own set of linguistic rules. The history and development of English are presented in a way which will encourage you to compare it with other languages you already know or are learning.

From 1990 every school student in the UK will have to learn a foreign language for five years. The study of a foreign language is easier and more interesting if your mind is open to the world of languages in general.

The **World Languages Project** introduces you to languages, the world of language and the languages of the world.

ACKNOWLEDGMENTS

The publishers would like to thank the following for their permission to reproduce copyright material:

Al Hayat for the use of their logo; The American Association of Endodontists for the extract from 'The pH of Local Anaesthetics/Calcium Hydroxide Solutions' by D G Stamos, G C Haasch and H Gerstein from the *Journal of Endodontics* Vol 11, no 6, June 1985; Amnesty International for an advertisement for a Research Team Assistant – Middle East; Artemis Publishers for the illustration 'Musca' from *Orbis Pictus Latinus* by Hermann Koller © Artemis Verlag, Zürich and München 1976; Bodleian Library for a section of the M S Digby 23 *Chanson de Roland*, Fol. 43 lines 2366–2382; British Petroleum for use of oil production statistics published in the *BP Statistical Review of World Energy*, June 1988; the St Brides Printing Library for the illustration of the printing work by Abraham von Werdt of Nuremberg; Canvas Holidays for the advertisement for 'Summer Jobs Abroad'; Der Esperantist for use of their title logo; La Brita Esperantista for use of their logo; Esperanto Asocio de Britujo for use of the cover from 'Esperanto: First Lesson'; Heroldo de Esperanto for use of their title logo; Her Majesty's Stationery Office for the extract from the *Education Reform Act* 1988; ILEA Research and Statistics Branch for the 1987 Language Census, *ILEA News* 26 November 1987; The Independent for the extract from 'What children need to know at various levels of testing' *The Independent* 30 April 1988; Japana Esperanto-Instituto for use of the logo for *La Revuo Orienta*; London East Anglian Group for extracts from past A Level examination papers (Bulgarian, Chinese, Dutch, Gujurati, Hebrew, Hindi, Polish, Portuguese, Serbo-Croat, Tamil, Turkish, Urdu.) p 10; Leeds Postcards for the postcard 'Les nits sont fredes' originally published 1936 by PSU-UGT Ediciones del Secretariat d'Agitacio i Propaganda, from the collection of Robin Langdon-Davies; London East Anglian Group for the extract from the GCSE examination paper, 1989: Bengali; De Nederlandsche Bank for the reproduction of a Tien Gulden banknote; Open University for use of the Eckert IV World Map Projection; Phileleftheros for the use of their logo; Pravda for the use of an extract from *Pravda* and for the use of their logo; Princeton University Press for the poem 'Three red pigeons' from *George Seferis: Collected Poems 1924–1955* trans., eds., Edmund Keeley and Philip Sherrard, Copyright © 1967 Princeton University Press; The Times for extracts from 'Back to Grammar', *The Times* 30 April 1988; the School of Oriental and African Studies, University of London for specimens of Balinese, Batik, Javanese and Sanskrit; VAAP for permission to use the logo *Sovietskaya Rossiya*.

Every effort has been made to trace copyright material reproduced in this book. Any rights not acknowledged here will be acknowledged in subsequent printings if notice is given to the publishers.

The authors and publishers would like to thank the following for permission to reproduce photographs:
J Allan Cash for the photos on pages 39, 46 left, 52, 53, 61 top, 88 top, 88 middle left, 88 bottom left, 88 bottom right, 98 left, 98 right, 101 left, 107 left, 107 right, 108 middle left, 114 top right, 114 middle, 115 middle; Barnaby's Picture Library for the photos on pages 9, 39 bottom middle, 108 right, 114 top left; Anne Bolt for the photo on page 13; Trustees of the British Museum for the photo on page 46 right, and for both photos on page 47; French Government Tourist Office for the photo on page 35; Sally and Richard Greenhill for the photo on page 15; Hong Kong Government Office for the photos on pages 41 and 61 bottom; Hulton Picture Company for the photos on pages 54, 97, 101 right; Hutchinson Library for the photo on page 120; Jewish Museum for the photo on page 56; Liverpool Museum for the photo on page 34; Panos Pictures/David Reed for the photo on page 64; Panos Pictures/Sean Prague for the photos on pages 39 top right and 108 top; Popperfoto for the photos on pages 88 middle right and 90; Ronald Sheridan, Ancient Art and Architecture Collection for the photo on page 99; Topham Picture Library for the photo on page 115 top.

Special thanks are due to the following:
G M Awbery of the Welsh Folk Museum for her assistance in documenting the spread of Celtic languages in Great Britain and Ireland; Catherine L Booth for her translation of a section of *Beowulf*, page 65; Martin Daly of SOAS for his help in supplying specialist foreign language texts; Patty Rowe and Wei Yue Hong for supplying Chinese script.

CONTENTS

1 Languages and You

Пролетарии всех стран, соединяйтесь!

Коммунистическая партия Советского Союза

ПРАВДА

Орган Центрального Комитета КПСС

Газета основана
5 мая 1912 года
В. И. ЛЕНИНЫМ

Четверг, 19 января 1989 года   Цена 4 коп.

№ 19 (25737)

ЗЕМНЫЕ ЗАБОТЫ АВИАТОРОВ

Прибыльное предприятие

За рубежом

Обсуждая перспективы реформы

Не сошлись во мнениях

Волнения в Майами

¡GRAN EXITO!

Cine PALAFOX
IL MEJOR CINE DE EUROPA, CON LOS MAXIMOS ADELANTOS DEL CINE MODERNO

ALPHAVILLE
EQUIPADO CON SISTEMA DOLBY STEREO
V.O. SUBTITULADA

CINE ARLEQUIN
San Bernardo 5 y 7

CINE CRISTAL

9 NOMINACIONES
A LOS OSCARS DE HOLLYWOOD

MEJOR PELICULA
MEJOR DIRECTOR

MEJOR GUION ADAPTADO
MEJOR DIRECCION ARTISTICA
MEJOR FOTOGRAFIA
MEJOR MONTAJE
MEJOR VESTUARIO
MEJOR SONIDO
MEJOR PARTITURA ORIGINAL

UN FILM DE BERNARDO BERTOLUCCI

EL ULTIMO EMPERADOR

Iberoamericana DISTRIBUCION

OPPORTUNITIES IN MARKETING FOR LINGUISTS

...RLDWIDE CONFERENCE ...NAGEMENT GROUP requires 2 ...aduates (or equivalent) to join this ...namic and fast-growing industry.

...hese openings will suit determined ...ersons seeking challenging careers who ...re free to travel regularly in Europe.

Fluency is required in either: German, Italian, French or a Scandinavian language (any mother tongue).

Preference will be shown to applicants with Qualifications/Background/ Experience in Marketing/Market Research/Sale...

Rin...

CLC LAN...

INTERGRUPP SERVICE, S.A.

Empresa Nacional de Servicios

necesita para ampliar
su plantilla

SECRETARIAS BILINGÜES

(INGLÉS, FRANCÉS Y ALEMÁN)

SE REQUIERE:
● Experiencia mínima de 3 años
● Nacionalidad española.
● Incorporación inmediata.

Interesadas, ...

TEACH YOURSELF
Turkish
Cassette to accompany...

TEACH YOURSELF
Arabic
Cassette to accompany
the Teach Yourself
coursebook by
J.R. Smart
Hodder and Stoughton

RESEARCH TEAM ASSISTANT — MIDDLE EAST

...xed Term Contract — February to July 1989)

...nesty International requires a Research Team ...sistant to provide secretarial assistance to one of ...r research teams working on human rights in the ...ddle East.

...ndidates must have excellent secretarial skills ...d be able to work under pressure as part of a ...m. Excellent English essential, Arabic an asset. ...ary £10,360 pa (pro rata).

...sing date for applications: 20th January 1989.

...r further information and an application form, ...se contact:

...sonnel Office, Amnesty International
...ternational Secretariat
...ton Street
...don WC1X 8DJ,
...ited Kingdom
...5
...one)

amnesty International

SUMMER JOBS ABROAD

If you are looking for the job of a lifetime, come and work for us as a Resident Campsite Courier on one of our campsites in Europe. You need to be hardworking, practical, responsible and have knowlege of a major European language (French, German, Spanish or Italian). W... are looking for applicants aged between 18 and 25, available from April to mid-July or mid-July to late September. Children's Courier... Watersports Couriers and Flying Squads are also required. Plea... ...Waterspo... application form quoting ref: G3

Courier Department,
...HOLIDAYS LTD.,
...ord, Herts SC14 1DY.

...nvas Holidays

Allô! Allô!

Rosa Martin and Martyn Ellis

Oiga
POR FAVOR

Cassette B
Listening and Speaking Activities
for Spanish GCSE

Español
Mundial 1

Sol Garson and Barbara Hill

N'hésitez pas!

Denise Jolivet
Jeanette Kitteringham

Edward Arnold

6

The pH of Local Anesthetic/Calcium Hydroxide Solutions

El pH de las Mezclas de Anestesicos Locales con Hidróxido de Calcio

Daniel G. Stamos, DDS, Gregory C. Haasch, DDS, and Harold Gerstein, DDS

An in vitro investigation was conducted to ascertain whether mixing local anesthetics with calcium hydroxide had any effect on the final pH of the calcium hydroxide solution. Three saturated solutions were prepared using normal saline, lidocaine, or mepivacaine mixed with calcium hydroxide. The pH of each solution was measured using a digital pH meter. No significant difference in pH was found when calcium hydroxide was mixed with normal saline, lidocaine, or mepivacaine.

Se realizó una investigación para determinar si la mezcla de anestésicos locales con hidróxido de calcio tenia consecuencias sobre el pH final de la solución de hidróxido de calcio. Se prepararon tres soluciones saturadas usando solución fisiológica, lidocaina, o mepivacaina mezclada con hodróxido de calcio. El pH de las soluciones se midió con un medidor digital de pH. Los resultados demostraron que no hubo diferencias significativas en el pH del hidróxido de calcio mezclado con solución fisiológica, lidocaina o mepivacaina.

HOW GOOD IS YOUR EAR?

Record your answers to the following exercises in your books.

A You are going to hear regional variations in English, rather than national ones. Can you identify them from the list below?

Cockney
Birmingham
Liverpudlian
Geordie
West Country
Yorkshire

B Listen now to a passage being read by two English people. What can you tell about these people?

BACK TO GRAMMAR

Many of the linguistic insights of the sixties and seventies were not only useful, but also true. The old insistence that the only Queen's English worth teaching was the formal, written kind, and that the correct way to speak it when invited to in class was Received Pronunciation as spoken in the great public schools was wrong, socially divisive and wasteful.

Generations of children were taught to hate grammar or be ashamed of their language as they spoke it. It was a leap forward to recognize that there are as many registers of English, each with its own grammar and rules and idioms, and that what is right or appropriate in one can be wrong or inappropriate in another.

But the pendulum swung too far. That is what pendulums do. The sillier the enthusiasts for the liberalization of English teaching adopted a creed of "creativity" and relativism in which anybody's English was as good as anybody else's. This was a rousing egalitarian slogan, but palpable nonsense. Instead of a meagre diet of nothing but spelling and parsing, they gave only the cream — creative writing and self-expression.

There was no grammar, no spelling, no rules. The illogicality (and hypocrisy) of the anti-grammarian dyslexicographers is demonstrated by their submissions to the Kingman committee, which are written in impeccable if not very lively Standard English. To deny this vital skill to their pupils would be robbing children and a wicked waste.

Below: targets set for pupils and teachers of English in schools, published in *The Times* and the *Independent*, 29 April 1988

What children need to know at various levels of testing

For 11-year-olds
- Read aloud, showing by use of intonation that they understand what is being read.
- Make a brief, but systematic, observation of ways in which dialect forms differ from those of Standard English.

For 16-year-olds
- Speak in Standard English, using their own accents provided these do not impair comprehension by other English speakers.

C You are now going to hear four people speaking. Can you identify why the language used by each speaker is different?

D Now listen to the same sentence being read in English by ten different people. Can you identify the country of each speaker? Choose from the list given below.

**England   Australia   South Africa   Jamaica   Ireland   Wales   Scotland
Canada   USA   New Zealand**

"I'm mad about my flat!"

"I'm mad about my flat!"

Can you think of other words that speakers from the various English speaking countries would use differently from speakers in the United Kingdom?

E You are now going to hear twenty people all saying the following in their own language:

> My name is . . .
> I live in . . . (name of a city).
> I do not speak English.

Decide which language you think you are hearing from the two choices given for each of the following:

1 **Italian** or **Bengali**	2 **Arabic** or **French**
3 **Welsh** or **Japanese**	4 **Polish** or **Spanish**
5 **Russian** or **Punjabi**	6 **Zulu** or **Turkish**
7 **Yoruba** or **Greek**	8 **Swahili** or **German**
9 **Tagalog** or **Ukranian**	10 **Cantonese** or **Portuguese**
11 **German** or **Polish**	12 **Hungarian** or **Swedish**
13 **French** or **Navajo**	14 **Farsi** or **Dutch**
15 **Japanese** or **Italian**	16 **Greek** or **Finnish**
17 **Twi** or **Hindi**	18 **Swedish** or **Swahili**
19 **Bulgarian** or **Malay**	20 **Nepali** or **Czech**

Suleyman Mosque, Istanbul, Turkey

LONDON EAST ANGLIAN GROUP

EAST ANGLIAN EXAMINATIONS BOARD

LONDON REGIONAL EXAMINING BOARD

UNIVERSITY OF LONDON SCHOOL EXAMINATIONS COUNCIL

GCSE EXAMINATION

FRIDAY 9th JUNE 1989—AFTERNOON

সিলেবাসের নাম	Syllabus Title	BENGALI	বাংলা
পত্রসংখ্যা	Paper Number	Paper 4 – Further Writing	চতুর্থ পত্র – উচ্চ পর্যায়ের রচনা
সময় –	Time allowed	1 hour 45 minutes	পৌনে দুই ঘন্টা

Write your answers in the separate answer book provided.

Answer *both* questions in Section A and *one* question from Section B.

তোমার উত্তরগুলি নির্দিষ্ট উত্তরপত্রে লিখবে ।

'ক' বিভাগের উভয় প্রশ্নের উত্তর লিখতে হবে এবং 'খ' বিভাগের যে কোন একটি প্রশ্নের উত্তর লিখবে ।

beba **ÁGUAS DE CARVALHELHOS**
PUREZA NO PALADAR
ÁGUAS MINERO MEDICINAIS E DE MESA COM E SEM GÁS

等候：置酒管待两个公人领了公文，监押宋江到州衙前。

当下两个公人领了公文，赍发了些银两，

太公唤宋江到僻静处叮嘱道：「我知江州是个好去处，

你可宽心守耐。我自使四郎来望你。盘缠，有便人常常

倘或他们下山来劫夺你入夥，切不可依随他，教人笑做不

孩儿，路上慢慢地去。天可怜见，早得回来，父子团圆做

Γιά νἆσαι ῞Ελληνας, δέν ἀρκεῖ νά μ

Πῶς ἐννοῶ τήν ἐλευθερία τοῦ ἀτό

Ταξιδεύοντας σ' ἄγνωστ

῾Η τυραννία τοῦ χρήματος

Προξενιά, κι ἄλλοι ἐφιάλτες

Σταδιοδρομία -τ' ἀγαπητό αι

Evler, insanla
alışkanlıklar ve
meydana getirdikleri
bölümünü geçirdikleri
krallarının başkenti oli
yapılışları günümüzden en
uzanmaktadır.

boyu edindikleri kültür,
inden doğan ihtiyaçla
amlarının büyük bir
cmişte Kapadokya
tarihi evlerinin
öncesine kadar

W którym kraju najchę
dlaczego?

Do jakiego stop
że człowiek sta

Jakie no
sz

f niet zonder
wanneer
liet en
in de
olnikiem
ial(a)byś wi
owinno

De schrijver F. Bordewijk bescho
ironie als een dilettant. Missc
men denkt aan het aanzienli
wanneer men de reputatie
Nederlandse letteren van

公同兄弟
包裹，
地使钱
去正从
此一节

भारतवर्ष की सभी भाषाएँ या तो प्रत्यक्ष रू
अप्रत्यक्ष रूप से संस्कृत से निकली हैं। गुजराती, मराठी और
की तो लिपियाँ भी देवनागरी से मिलती जुलती हैं। यद्य
दक्षिणी भारत की भाषाओं की लिपियाँ बिल्कुल भिन्न हैं, परंतु
फिर भी उनमें संस्कृत शब्दों की बहुत अधिकता है। अरबी और
फ़ारसी के शब्द भी
रंतु उनमें सं
ीय भाषाओं में कुछ न कुछ मिलते हैं।
तनी अधिकता नहीं होती जितनी

Arhitektura u gradovima.

Kakve su razlike između predstava u pozorištu
bioskopu?

Srpskohrvatski — jedan ili dva jezika?
evropskim zemljama?

Šta nudi Jugoslavija

Priroda u Jugoslav

Nade današnje

• ऋणेक दिवस गया. समी सांज हती. मास्तर शाळाऐथी आवीने
चा अनावता हता, त्यां ऐमना मकानमां विशाख्या आवी.
पोताने विना कारणु तमाच्या मारनार स्त्रीने, पोताने घेर विना
कारणु आवेशी जोई, मास्तरने नवाई लागी. 'आवो अहीन! चा
लेशो?' ऋव

Всяко зърно поотделно бе завито в книжка.
Стоил гледа полето и бави отговора си.
— Жалният вой на бездомните псета към луната.
Аз искам да напиша днес поема.

אֲנִי צִפּוֹר מֵתָה
אֲנִי צִפּוֹר מֵתָה,
צִפּוֹר אַחַת שְׁמֵתָה
צִפּוֹר עוֹטָה מ'
בִּלְכְתִּי, לֵ' מ
פָּתַח אֲפַפְתֻנִי
חֵי עוֹלָמִים
בְּשׁוּק שׁוֹקֵק
רַק אַתָּה קָם•
בְּשׁוּק שׁוֹקֵק צִפּוֹר מֵרַדָּה עִם שִׁיר
נִסְתָּר•

Languages Questionnaire

The last census in Inner London showed that 172 languages are spoken amongst the pupils in its schools. Many other cities in the UK also have pupils who speak or understand languages other than

ILEA pupils speak 172 different languages – here they are

World of languages

AS ILEA News reported last week, the latest research figures show that London pupils speak a total of 172 different languages.

But what languages are they? We thought you might like to know, so here is the full list – courtesy of ILEA's Research and Statistics Branch.

The figures on the right-hand side show the number of speakers of each language, and the code-letters on the left indicate in which part of the world each is spoken.

(WA)	ABUA	(1)
(NA)	ACHOLI	(4)
(WA)	ADANGME	(23)
(SA)	AFRIKAANS	(23)
(WA)	AKAN	(25)
(E)	ALBANIAN	(3)
(NA)	AMHARIC	(62)
(ME)	ARABIC	(3,067)
(MR)	ARAMAIC	(3)
(ME)	ARMENIAN	(24)
(WA)	ASANTE	(59)
(I)	ASSAMESE	(1)
(ME)	ASSYRIAN	(9)
(ME)	AZARI	(1)
(EA)	BALI	(1)
(I)	BALUCHI	(7)
(WA)	BARIBA	(1)
(WA)	BASSA	(1)
(SA)	BEMBA	(16)
(I)	BENGALI	(16,976)
(NA)	BERBER	(8)
(SEA)	BISLAMA	(1)
(E)	BULGARIAN	(72)
(SEA)	BURMESE	(20)
(E)	CATALAN	(1)
(SEA)	CEBUANO	(5)
(WA)	CHE	(2)
(SA)	CHEWA/NYANJA	(25)
(SEA)	CHINESE	(4,325)
(E)	CZECH	(41)
(WA)	DAGARI	(1)
(WA)	DAGBANE	(4)
(E)	DANISH	(35)
(NA)	DINKA	(10)
(E)	DUTCH	(92)
(WA)	EDO/BINI	(29)
(WA)	EFIK/IBIBIO	(24)
(WA)	EMAI	(2)
(WA)	EWE	(46)
(WA)	FANG	(3)
(WA)	FANTE	(273)
(FE)	FIJIAN	(6)
(E)	FINNISH	(49)
(E)	FLEMISH	(14)
(WA)	FON	(1)
(E)	FRENCH	(2,357)
(EA)	FRUAE	(1)
(WA)	FULANI	(2)
(WA)	GA	(340)
(E)	GAELIC/IRISH	(170)
(E)	GAELIC/SCOTTISH	(1)
(EA)	GALLA	(3)
(WA)	GANE	(1)
(E)	GERMAN	(279)
(WA)	GONJA	(2)
(E)	GREEK	(2,596)
(I)	GUJERATI	(3,930)
(WA)	GURMA	(12)
(NA)	HAUSA	(45)
(SEA)	HAWAIIAN	(1)
(ME)	HEBREW	(384)
(I)	HINDI	(648)
(E)	HUNGARIAN	(86)
(WA)	IBO	(755)
(E)	ICELANDIC	(8)
(WA)	IDOMA	(3)
(WA)	IGBIRA	(3)
(WA)	IGEDE	(5)
(WA)	IJO	(24)
(SEA)	ILOCANO	(49)
(SEA)	ILONGO	(1)
(SEA)	INDONESIAN	(12)
(WA)	ISHAN	(6)
(E)	ITALIAN	(1,889)
(SEA)	JAPANESE	(140)
(SEA)	JAVANESE	(1)
(WA)	KAJE	(3)
(I)	KASHMIRI	(1)
(EA)	KEHI	(5)
(WA)	KHANA	(1)
(SEA)	KHMER	(16)
(I)	KHASI	(6)
(WA)	KIKONGO	(2)
(EA)	KIKUYU	(15)
(I)	KONKANI	(38)
(SEA)	KOREAN	(57)
(WA)	KPELLE	(2)
(WA)	KRIO	(52)
(EA)	KUMA	(1)
(ME)	KURDISH	(34)
(I)	LAHNDA	(1)
(SEA)	LAO	(9)
(SA)	LINGALA	(9)
(E)	LITHUANIAN	(1)
(SA)	LOZI	(2)
(EA)	LUGANDA	(107)
(EA)	LUO	(4)
(E)	MACEDONIAN	(4)
(SEA)	MALAY	(150)
(I)	MALAYALAM	(19)
(WA)	MALINKE	(9)
(E)	MALTESE	(358)
(I)	MARATHI	(13)
(EA)	MASABA	(1)
(WA)	MENDE	(27)
(SA)	NDEBELE	(7)
(I)	NEPALI	(42)
(E)	NORWEGIAN	(30)
(SA)	NSENGA	(1)
(NA)	NUER	(1)
(WA)	NYANG	(1)
(EA)	NYARI	(1)
(WA)	NZEMA	(7)
(WA)	ORING	(1)
(I)	ORIYA	(1)
(I)	PATUA	(1)
(SEA)	PAMPANGAN	(31)
(I)	PANJABI	(3,200)
(I)	PASHTO	(75)
(ME)	PERSIAN	(582)
(E)	POLISH	(582)
(E)	PORTUGUESE	(1,951)
(WA)	ROBA	(2)
(E)	ROMANSCH	(1)
(E)	ROMANY	(7)
(EA)	RUANDA	(3)
(E)	RUMANIAN	(9)
(EA)	RUNYANKORE	(4)
(E)	RUSSIAN	(24)
(EA)	RUTORO	(5)
(I)	SANTALI	(1)
(E)	SERBO-CROAT	(219)
(SA)	SHONA	(57)
(I)	SINDHI	(23)
(I)	SINGHALESE	(170)
(E)	SLOVAK	(2)
(E)	SLOVENE	(5)
(NA)	SOMALI	(158)
(SA)	SOTHO	(4)
(E)	SPANISH	(3,229)
(EA)	SWAHILI	(138)
(SA)	SWAZI	(1)
(E)	SWEDISH	(73)
(SEA)	TAGALOG	(968)
(I)	TAMIL	(370)
(I)	TELUGA	(1)
(WA)	TEMNE	(16)
(SEA)	THAI	(132)
(SEA)	TIBETAN	(1)
(NA)	TIGRE	(5)
(NA)	TIGRINYA	(107)
(WA)	TIV	(8)
(SA)	TONGA	(5)
(SEA)	TONGAN	(3)
(SA)	TSWANA	(8)
(SA)	TUMBUKA	(2)
(ME)	TURKISH	(4,495)
(WA)	TWI	(947)
(E)	UKRAINIAN	(10)
(WA)	UKUANI	(1)
(I)	URDU	(3,808)
(WA)	URHOBO	(68)
(SEA)	VIETNAMESE	(1,028)
(E)	WELSH	(19)
(WA)	WIN	(1)
(WA)	WOLOF	(50)
(SA)	XHOSA	(5)
(SEA)	YAO	(3)
(WA)	YAUNDE	(1)
(E)	YIDDISH	(2)
(WA)	YORUBA	(2,031)
(SA)	ZULU	(8)

Unidentified from:
GHANA (73)
INDIA (5)
NIGERIA (76)
SIERRE LEONE (2)

KEY TO AREA CODES

I – India, Pakistan, Bangladesh, Sri Lanka etc.
ME – Middle East
E – Europe
SEA – South East Asia
WA – West Africa
NA – North Africa
EA – East Africa
SA – Southern Africa

1987 Language Census, ILEA Research and Statistics Branch

English. Some will use their mother tongue all the time at home and many will be literate in it. Others may just understand it and only respond in English. Refer to the World Map accompanying this book to locate the regions where these languages are spoken.

F Which languages are spoken or just understood by your classmates? If your classmates speak languages other than English, find out where these languages are spoken and if they are the official languages of those countries.

French is the official language of France, as well as one of the official languages in Belgium, Switzerland and Canada. It is spoken in New Orleans in the USA, Sark in the Channel Islands, the Central African Republic, Chad, Martinique, French Guinea, French Guyana, Mali, parts of Morocco and Algeria and in many other African countries where it is not necessarily the only official language.

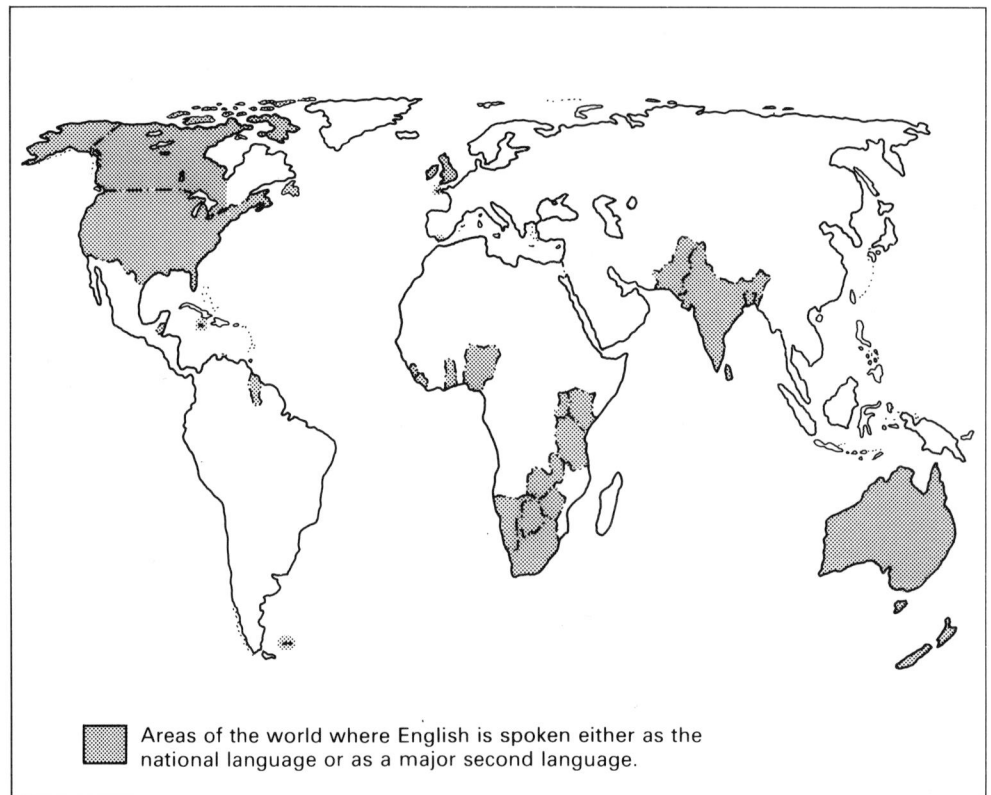

Areas of the world where English is spoken either as the national language or as a major second language.

G Consider also the countries where English is the official or majority language. Can you make one list of countries where English is the official language and another of countries where English is widely used?

Many languages are spoken in countries where they are not the national language and in some cases they may not even be considered the official languages in the regions where they are spoken. The status given to these languages is often dependent on political considerations.

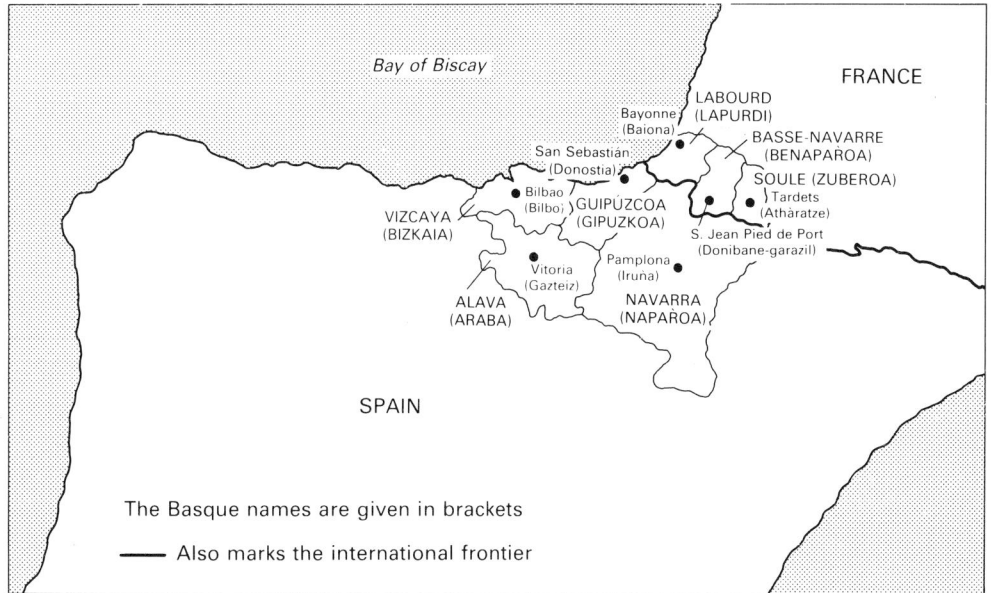

Basque provinces of France and Spain

Gibraltar with Spain across the airstrip

For example, between 1939 and 1975 Euskara (Basque) was denied official status in the Basque region of Spain and its use repressed for political reasons. Basque and Spanish are both now the official languages of the region.

Why has this change taken place?

Consider this second example. The majority of the people in Gibraltar will speak Spanish as their first language, yet when it comes to reading and writing most would choose to do so in English and find it easier. This is because English is the official language in education, the media and in government affairs.

Find out why this is so.

The Indian rupee bill has information printed in thirteen languages. Why is this so?

All children in Bulgaria learn Russian from an early age. Why is this so?

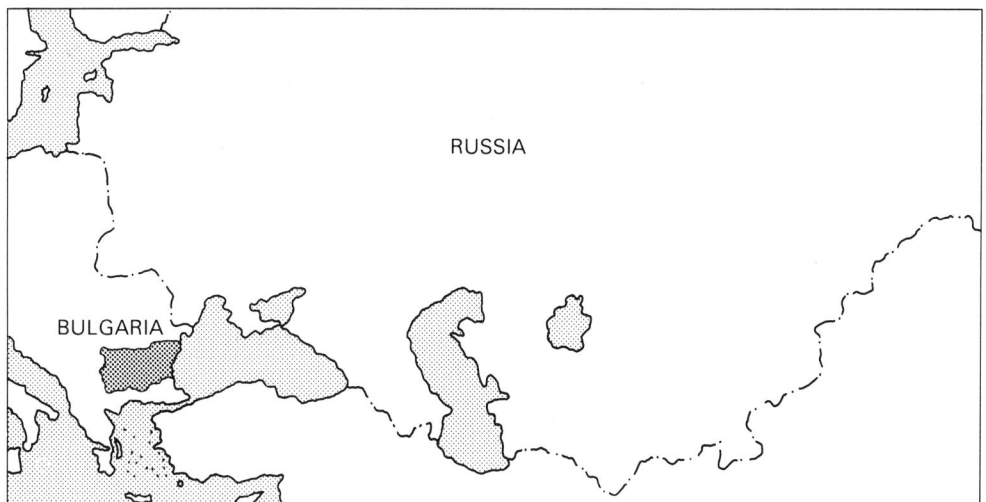

Some of you may have relatives who speak languages other than English. Sometimes you may tune into a foreign radio station or you may hear your schoolfriends speaking another language. Do you ever watch films with subtitles? If you have contact with tourists in your area, do you recognise the languages they speak?

Explain the circumstances in which you sometimes listen to languages other than English.

If you look around carefully at home, in the street or in shops, you will surely come across material written in other languages. These may be in the Roman script or another. You may have books or comics in other languages. You will probably have seen instruction leaflets in more than one language. Have you noticed food wrappers with information printed in various languages?

Which languages do you often see and recognise in their written form and where?

It is very likely that your parents, at some time in their lives, have had to learn a foreign language. It may have been at school, for business purposes, for holiday use or because they have had to live in another country.

Who in your family has had to learn a foreign language and how well do they speak it?

The National Curriculum states that all pupils in Britain have to learn a 'modern foreign language' from the first to the fifth years of secondary education. In some cases pupils will choose to study two languages or there may be schemes at school where pupils start off with as many as three, and then specialise in either one or two. Non-European languages, as well as Latin and Greek, can also be studied in many secondary schools in Britain.

Extract from the Education Reform
Act, 1988
(a), (b) – core subjects
(a), (b), (c) – other foundation
subjects
Third key stage: 12–14 years
Fourth key stage: 15–16 years

(a) mathematics, English and science; and

(b) in relation to schools in Wales which are Welsh-speaking schools, Welsh.

(a) history, geography, technology, music, art and physical education;

(b) in relation to the third and fourth key stages, a modern foreign language specified in an order of the Secretary of State; and

(c) in relation to schools in Wales which are not Welsh-speaking schools, Welsh.

H Now consider the following questions:

1 Find out what languages are taught in your school. In what year can you start to study them and up to what level?

2 What other opportunities do you have, outside school, to learn another language?

3 Do many pupils in your school sit examinations in mother tongues other than English?

4 Which languages do you think are important for pupils in the United Kingdom to study?

5 Do you think you should have the opportunity to learn a language that does not use the Roman script?

6 Which languages would you like to learn? Why?

7 What opportunities do you have to either visit the countries where these languages are spoken or to meet with native speakers?

8 Why do you think the British have been so reluctant to learn languages?

9 How useful will the study of foreign languages be to you?

10 In which careers would ' languages' prove useful?

Britain is a multi-lingual nation. Some languages have been here for a long time, others have arrived more recently. Apart from English, we know that Welsh, Gaelic (Scotland and Ireland) and French in Sark (Channel Islands) are still widely spoken. There are still about twenty speakers of Manx (Isle of Man) but Cornish (Cornwall) has disappeared as a living language.

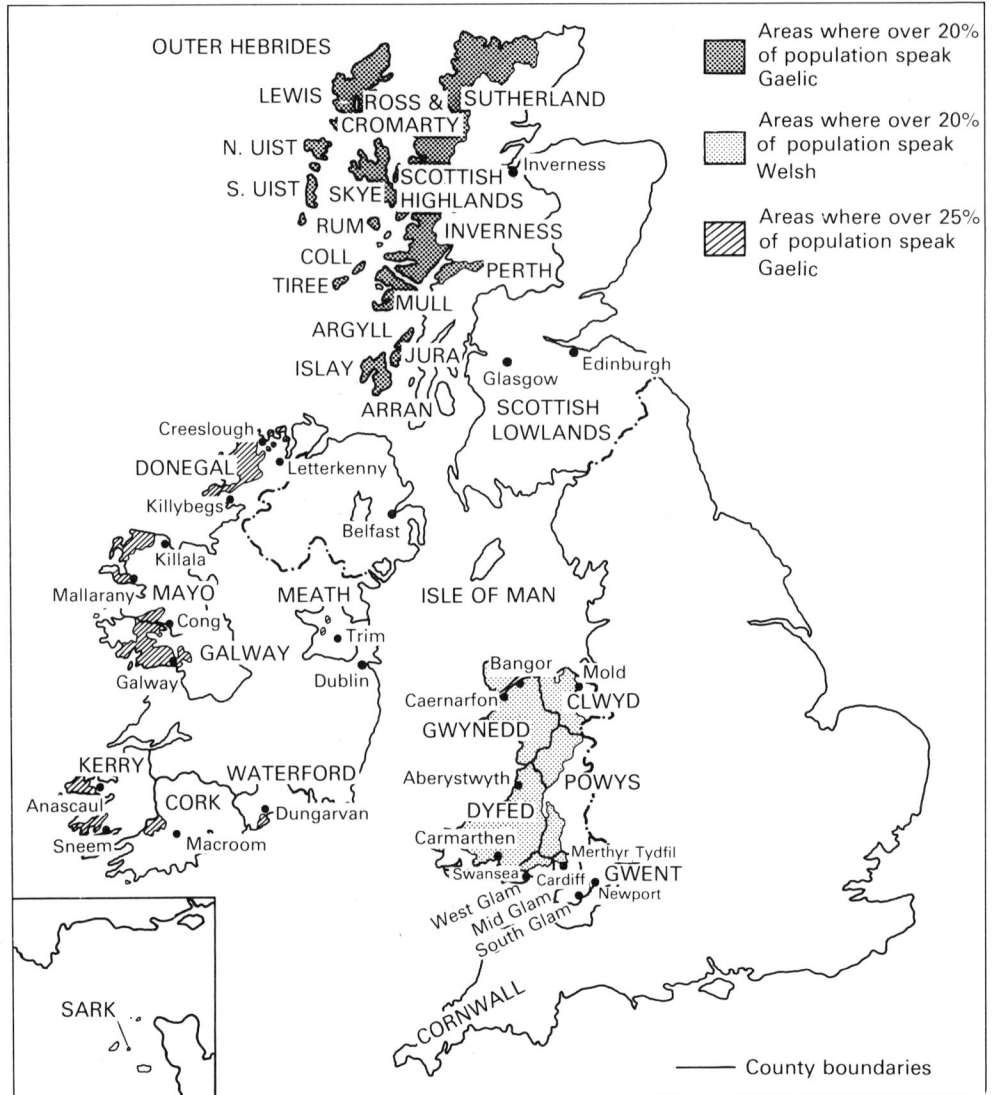

Map legend:
- Areas where over 20% of population speak Gaelic
- Areas where over 20% of population speak Welsh
- Areas where over 25% of population speak Gaelic
- —— County boundaries

Existing Welsh, Irish and Scots Gaelic first-language speaking areas within the United Kingdom and French speaking Sark in the Channel Islands

A walk through the streets of London or a ride in the tube will bring you into contact with many languages. Some of these foreign language speakers may be tourists but many others actually live in the United Kingdom. Refer back to the chart of the different languages spoken by pupils in schools in Inner London.

Some people think that once settled in Britain, people should learn English and not bother to continue using their mother tongue.

How fair is this?

Opinions on this matter vary and every situation is different, although one thing is certain: all children learn to speak English at school. Let us look at a number of different cases.

A Spanish couple come to London. They have no children but start a family once they are settled. If the children go to nursery, primary and secondary school, they will speak English just like any other Londoner. If the parents are working mostly with other Spaniards, as is often the case, they will continue to use more Spanish than English. The children will probably speak English all the time but will understand Spanish quite well. If their parents work in an environment that brings them into much closer contact with English, then Spanish will be used less at home. The parents may choose to send their children to Spanish language classes to ensure that they are bilingual. In such cases, both languages may be used at home. Often, the parents will speak Spanish whilst the children reply in English.

However, many couples arrive in Britain with children. It means that they are already used to speaking their own language at home. The older the children are when they start their schooling in Britain, the more years of English they have to make up for, and the more fluent they are in another language.

Should we say to these children that they must not continue to work and study in their mother tongue?

What would happen to you if you had to start learning the foreign language from its very basics and you were given no opportunity to continue to learn and improve your English?

How would you feel?

Let us suppose that for reasons of work in 1992, your parents needed to move to another European country.

What difficulties would you have with the foreign language?

---

❶ Consider the following:
Imagine your family is emigrating to Madrid for employment reasons and for an indefinite period of time. None of you has ever studied Spanish. You are fourteen and are to attend an ordinary Spanish state school.
Discuss the following:

1 Would you want to continue to speak English at home with your family?
2 Would you learn Spanish more quickly than your parents?
3 Give reasons for your choice of answer to Qn. 2.
4 Would you still read English books? What kind?
5 Would you still buy English newspapers? Which?
6 Would you try to watch English films on television?
7 Would you be interested in television programmes about the United Kingdom?
8 Would you still be writing to friends back in the UK after two years in Spain?
9 Would you celebrate festivals as you did in England? (e.g. presents on the 25 December?)
10 Would you attend religious services in English?
11 Would you try to mix with British expatriates?
12 Would you buy English foodstuffs?
13 Would you start cooking Spanish style?
14 Would you try to listen to English stations on the radio?

15 Would you maintain your interest in 'English' music?

16 Would you try to have your holidays in the UK?

17 If Spain played football against England which team would you support?

18 If Spain played football against Italy which team would you support?

19 Would you miss cricket?

20 If your brothers/sisters were born in Spain would you always speak English to them?

21 How difficult would you find the following at first?

    a shopping in a supermarket
    b opening a bank account
    c registering with the police
    d meeting the Headteacher with your parents
    e lessons at school

	LUNES	MARTES	MIÉRCOLES	JUEVES	VIERNES
9-10	INGLÉS / FRANCÉS	MATEMÁTICAS	MATEMÁTICAS	INGLÉS / FRANCÉS	INGLÉS / FRANCÉS
10-11	MATEMÁTICAS	FILOSOFÍA	INGLÉS / FRANCÉS	FILOSOFÍA	FÍSICA Y QUÍMICA
11-11,30		R E C	R E O		
11,30-12,30	HISTORIA	FÍSICA Y QUÍMICA	HISTORIA	FÍSICA Y QUÍMICA	MATEMÁTICAS
12,30-13,30	EDUCACIÓN FÍSICA	HISTORIA	EDUCACIÓN FÍSICA	MATEMÁTICAS	EDUCACIÓN FÍSICA
			TARDE		
15,30-16,30	LENGUA	LENGUA	LENGUA	LENGUA	LENGUA
16,30-17,30	DIBUJO	ESTUDIO PERSONAL	DIBUJO	ESTUDIO PERSONAL	DIBUJO

22 How much would you need to know to do the following?

    a make friends outside school.
    b go to a football match.
    c go to a restaurant.
    d clothes shopping.
    e go to the Post Office.
    f visit your doctor.
    g go to a parents' evening.
    h fill in an income tax form.

And finally:

23 What would you miss most about the UK?

24 What do you think you would learn from being in Spain?

25 Why do you think that you would recognise a lot of words in Spanish?

26 Do you think that special arrangements ought to be made for pupils in British schools who have come from abroad, to ensure that they can continue to learn their mother tongue? If you do, how would you organise it?

2 Languages of the World

LANGUAGE VARIETY

This chapter will give you information about the variety of languages spoken in the world today, how many languages are spoken and where. Before you read the information, let us think about the languages of the world.

A

1 How many languages do you think there are? Discuss with a partner and decide. Are there:
   a under 100
   b 100–200
   c 1,000–2,000
   d more than 4,000?

2 Now, without looking in any books, write down all the languages you can think of.

You may be surprised to learn that about 4,000 languages are spoken throughout the world. Some of these are only spoken in a small area, by a small number of people. In Australia, for example, where English is spoken as the main language, there are also more than 200 aboriginal languages, some spoken by as few as ten people. Another example of an area where English is the main language but where many other languages are spoken, is North America. There are around 400 American Indian languages in North and South America. Africa has even more variety, with many languages local to a small area only.

Some languages are spoken by hundreds of millions of people, spread over huge distances and some by groups living in small villages. Some are major world languages, used for international discussions and trade; some are known only in a small area within a country. In addition to these 4,000 world languages there are as many more *dialects*, which are varieties of the major languages. Of all these, about ten can be called major world languages, because they are spoken by more than one hundred million people. In fact, of all these thousands of languages and dialects, fewer than one hundred are spoken by ninety-five per cent of the world's population. The language spoken by the highest number of people is Chinese (Mandarin); China is the country with the highest population.

There are some countries where many different languages are spoken (e.g. more than 150 different 'languages' in India and 130 in the Soviet Union). When there are many languages in use in a country, one or more *national* languages have to be chosen and used for all *official work*.

What kind of work do you think this is? Why do you think this is necessary?

Some of the world's major languages are spoken or used in many different countries. English is the most widely spoken and is the official language of thirty-four different countries. It is not, however, spoken by the greatest number of people. Even though it is used in so many countries it does not have as many speakers as Chinese.

The following bar-chart shows the languages with the largest number of speakers.

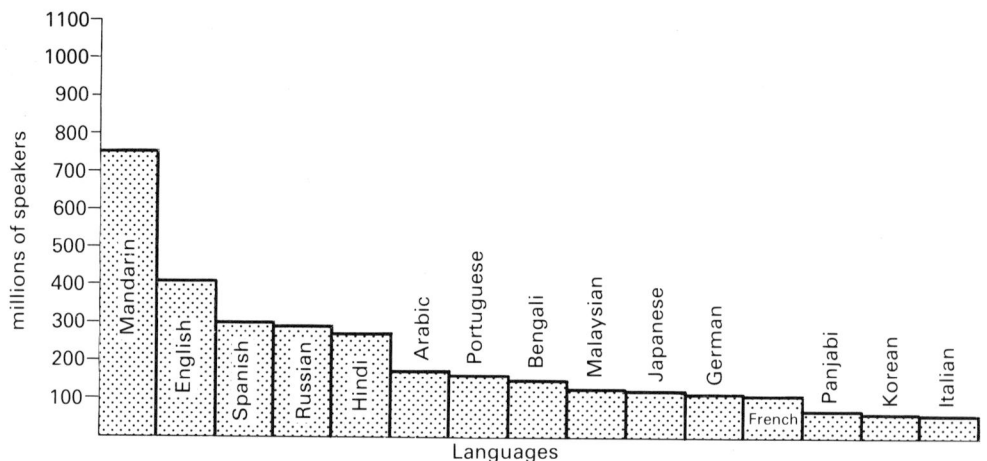

Numbers of speakers of major languages of the world, by population

B If you have speakers of other languages in your class, find out the names of these languages and where they are spoken. Arrange your answers in the form of a table in your exercise books. Use these headings to record your information in columns:

Name of language   Name of people who speak it   Where spoken

C 1 Look at the bar chart of languages with the most speakers. Are there any languages which surprise you?

Write this passage out in your books and fill in the gaps:

There are more than . . . . languages spoken in the world. If we include dialects too the number is . . . . The language with the largest number of speakers is . . . . It has not less than . . . . mother tongue speakers. The second language is . . . . and the number of speakers is . . . .

2 Write down the names and numbers of speakers of the other languages on the bar-chart.

Some people believe that all languages may have come from the same original tongue. It is more likely that there were several languages from which all known languages in the world today have grown. The original languages were used so far back in time that no one can be certain where they came from. Most of them have not left anything written and have vanished without a trace.

LANGUAGE FAMILIES

The languages of the world are grouped in families. As with human families, one can trace their family trees. We know that a language belongs to a certain family by studying how much it is like other members of the family and how it has been formed by the parent and grandparent languages.

Language families have spread through the world in different ways, as people have moved to new places. There may be several reasons why people move from their own home. They may travel to trade goods they have made or produce they have grown, or they may move to settle on new land when 'home places' become too crowded. Armies also carry languages to new places. Conquests have been one of the major ways in which languages have spread.

English belongs to one of the world's largest language families, called the Indo-European Family. The languages in this family are spoken by forty-nine per cent of the present world population. On the World Language Family Map you can see the area covered by this family of languages.

D 1 Find Pakistan, India and Bangladesh on the World Language Families Map, pp. 22–23. What is the key shading for this area?

2 Find Western and Eastern Europe. What shading is used for them on the map?

3 Find Latin America, North America, Australia and New Zealand and note the shading used here on the map. Why do you think two shades have been used? Look carefully at the key and discuss.

You have seen that the languages of the Indo-European family are spoken on the whole of the American continent, North and South. You have also seen that languages of the American Indian language families are spoken there. These are the languages which were spoken by the people who first lived in the lands of North and South America. Many of these languages are still spoken today. Have you heard of Navaho, Apache, Cree and Mohican? These languages get their names from the peoples who speak them.

The story of how five languages of Europe spread across the Atlantic Ocean is the story of how people from five countries in Europe moved to 'The Americas' to settle new lands, to conquer and take riches, and to trade. Spanish was the first European language to reach the continent of America, taken to Central then South America after Christopher Columbus crossed the Atlantic Ocean in 1492. Spanish was followed closely by Portuguese. French and English were subsequently taken to the West Indies, to Canada and to North America about fifty years later, with new voyages of exploration and the establishment of new settlements. Dutch arrived in the seventeenth century.

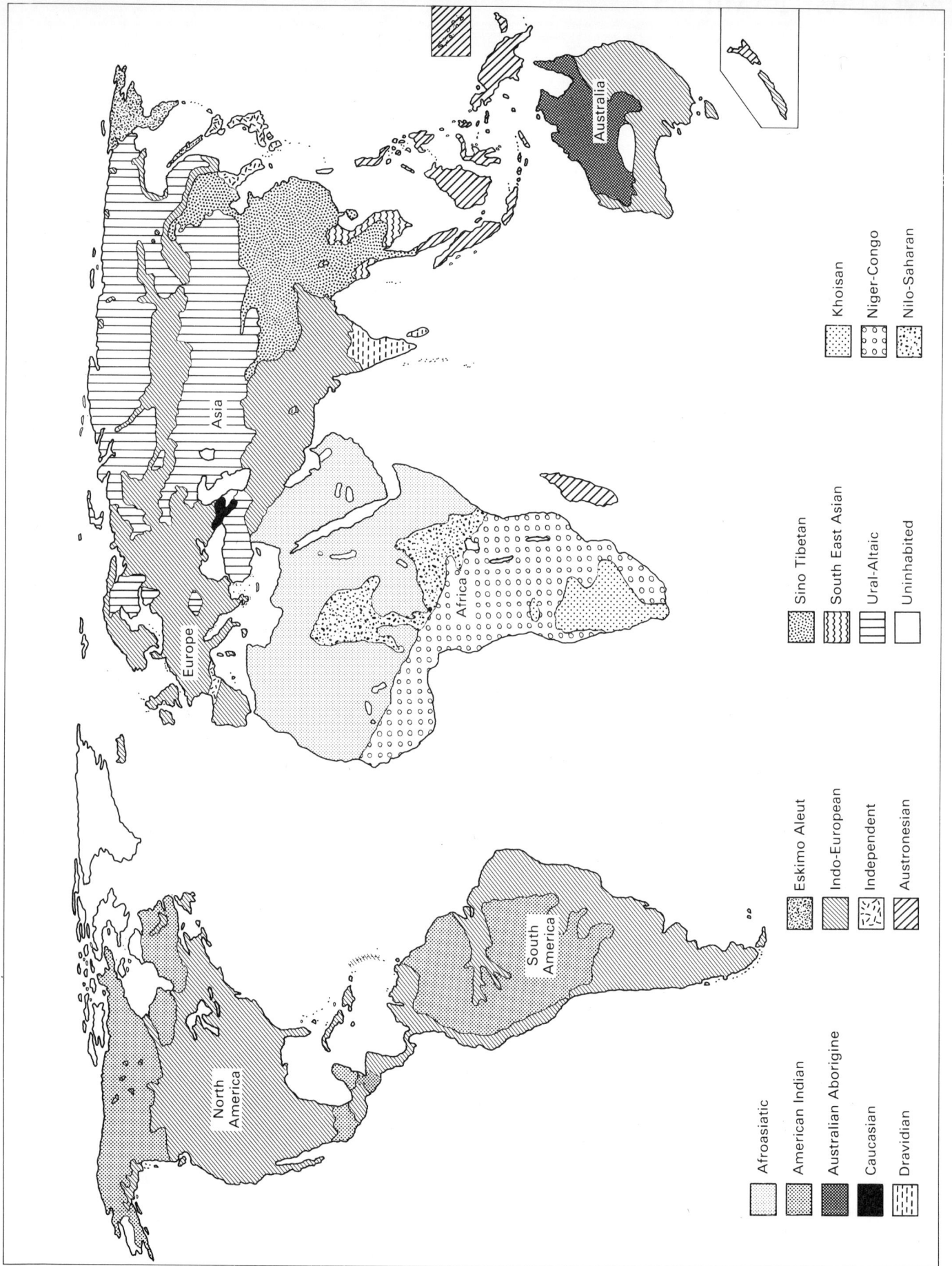

Legend:

Afroasiatic
American Indian
Australian Aborigine
Caucasian
Dravidian

Eskimo Aleut
Indo-European
Independent
Austronesian

Sino Tibetan
South East Asian
Ural-Altaic
Uninhabited

Khoisan
Niger-Congo
Nilo-Saharan

North America
South America
Europe
Asia
Africa
Australia

World Language Families Map, representing spread of families, not necessarily majority language family in any given area

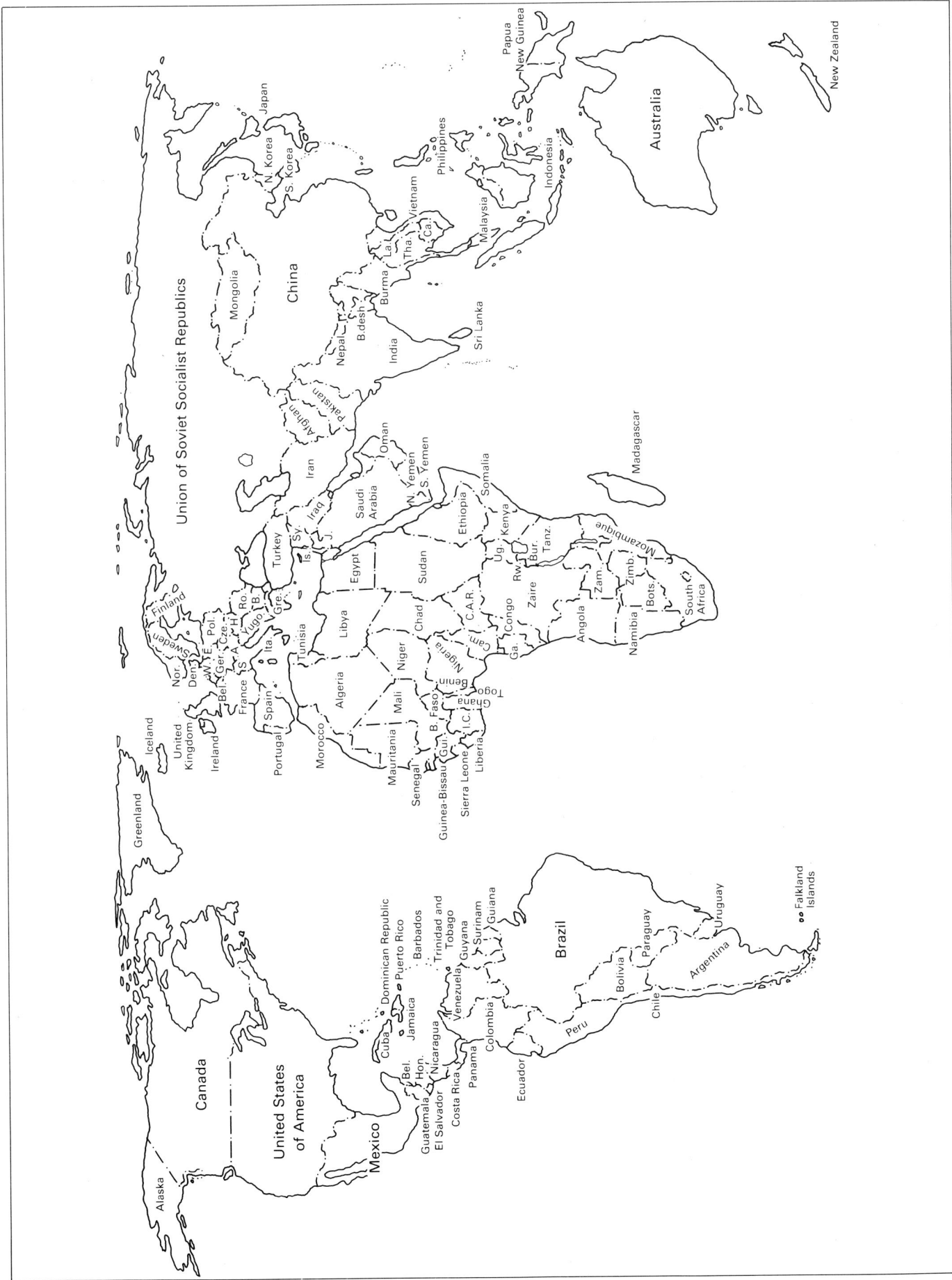

Alaska

Canada

United States
of America

Greenland

Mexico

Guatemala
El Salvador
Costa Rica
Panama

Bel.
Hon.
Nicaragua

Cuba
Jamaica
Dominican Republic
Puerto Rico
Barbados
Trinidad and
Tobago
Guyana
Surinam
Guiana

Colombia
Venezuela

Ecuador

Peru

Brazil

Bolivia
Paraguay

Chile
Argentina
Uruguay

Falkland
Islands

Iceland

United
Kingdom

Ireland

Portugal

Morocco

Mauritania
Senegal
Guinea-Bissau
Sierra Leone
Liberia

Gui.
B. Faso
I.C.

Nor.
Sweden
Den.

Finland

Union of Soviet Socialist Republics

Mongolia

China

N. Korea
S. Korea

Japan

Nepal
B.desh.

Burma
La.
Tha.
Vietnam
Ca.

Philippines

Malaysia

Indonesia

Papua
New Guinea

Australia

New Zealand

Afghan.
Pakistan

India

Sri Lanka

Iran

Iraq
Sy.
Is.
J.

Turkey

Saudi
Arabia

Oman

N. Yemen
S. Yemen

Madagascar

U.K.
Bel.
France
Spain

Ger.
S.
A.
Ita.

E.
Cze.
H.
Yugo.

Pol.
Ro.
B.
Gre.

Tunisia

Algeria

Libya

Egypt

Mali
Niger

Chad

Sudan

Ethiopia

Somalia

Benin
Togo
Ghana
Nigeria

Cam.
Ga.
Congo

C.A.R.

Zaire

Ug.
Rw.
Bur.

Kenya
Tanz.

Angola

Zam.

Namibia

Bots.
Zimb.

Mozambique

South
Africa

E Look up the voyages of discovery in a history book or in an encyclopedia. Find out about the following. Make notes on them. What did they do? When? What languages did they speak?

> Christopher Columbus
> Amerigo Vespucci
> Francis Drake
> Hernán Cortes
> Francisco Pisarro
> Ferdinand Magellan
> Jacques Cartier
> Montezuma
> The Inca
> Peter Stuyvesant

F To do this exercise you will need to look at the list on page 26 of major languages grouped in countries and to check on the world maps and the language family trees. Are these statements TRUE or FALSE?
1 Kwa is an Indo-European language.
2 Malay is an African language.
3 Turkish is an Indo-European language.
4 Japanese and Korean belong to the same language family.
5 Cantonese and Japanese belong to the same language family.

G Find out to which family the following languages belong, using the family trees and the language list:

> Panjabi   Chinese
> Tagalog   French
> Portuguese   Zulu

Here you can see three of the world's language families drawn as family trees. Not all the languages in each of the families have been included yet the number of branches gives you an idea of how many languages there can be in the families.

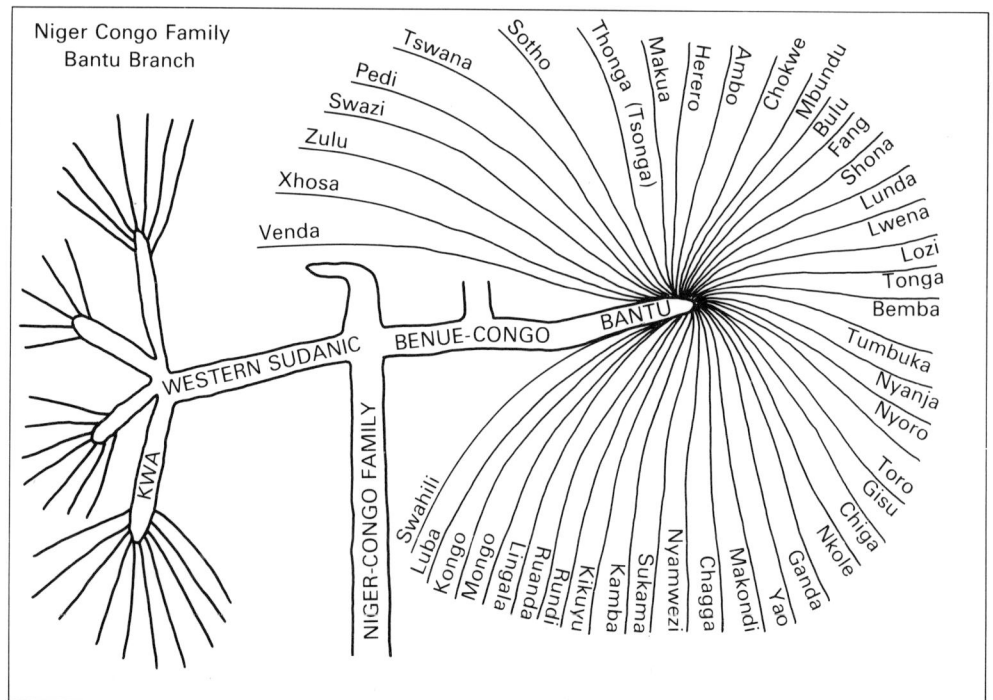

Niger Congo Family Bantu Branch

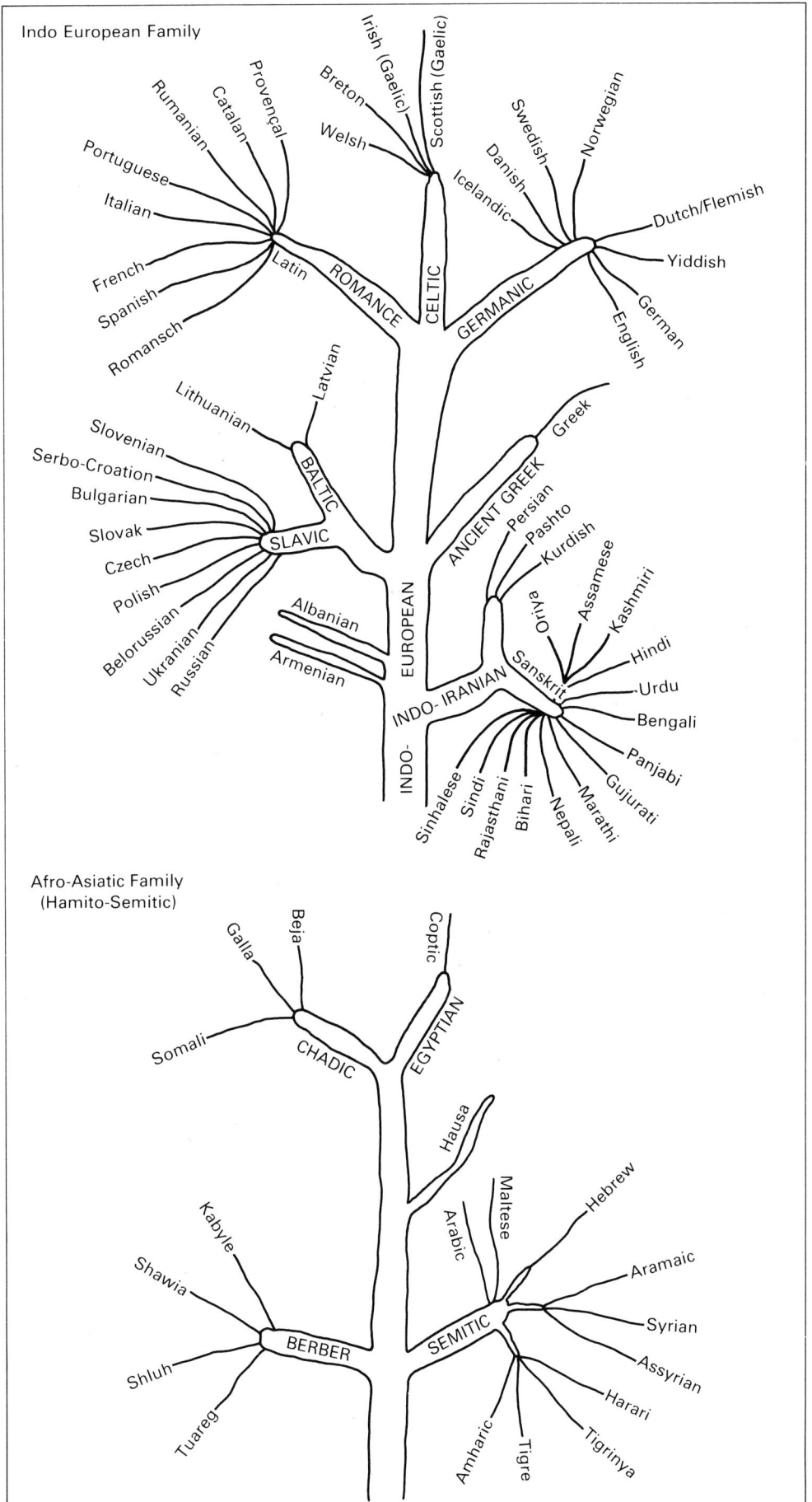

Indo European Family

Irish (Gaelic)
Scottish (Gaelic)
Breton
Welsh
Swedish
Norwegian
Danish
Icelandic
Dutch/Flemish
Yiddish
German
English
Rumanian
Catalan
Provençal
Portuguese
Italian
French
Spanish
Romansch
Latin
ROMANCE
CELTIC
GERMANIC

Lithuanian
Latvian
Slovenian
Serbo-Croation
Bulgarian
Slovak
Czech
Polish
Belorussian
Ukranian
Russian
SLAVIC
BALTIC
Albanian
Armenian

Greek
ANCIENT GREEK
Persian
Pashto
Kurdish
Oriya
Assamese
Kashmiri
Hindi
Urdu
Bengali
Panjabi
Gujurati
Marathi
Nepali
Bihari
Rajasthani
Sindi
Sinhalese
Sanskrit
INDO- IRANIAN

INDO- EUROPEAN

Afro-Asiatic Family
(Hamito-Semitic)

Galla
Beja
Coptic
Somali
CHADIC
EGYPTIAN
Hausa

Kabyle
Shawia
Arabic
Maltese
Hebrew
Aramaic
Syrian
Assyrian
Harari
Shluh
BERBER
SEMITIC
Tuareg
Amharic
Tigre
Tigrinya

Here is a list of some of the major languages in their family groups. It also shows countries where they are spoken. Which other families can you name?

FAMILY	COUNTRIES
Sino-Tibetan	
Thai (Siamese)	Thailand
Burmese	Burma
Tibetan	Tibet, N. China, Nepal
Mandarin (p'u-t'ung hun)	China
Mi	China
Wu	China
Yueh (Cantonese)	China
Uralic and Altaic	
Turkish	Turkey
Finnish	Finland
Hungarian	Hungary
Manchu	N. China
Independent	
Japanese	Japan
Korean	N. & S. Korea, China Japan, Soviet Union
Ainu	Japan
Dravidian	
Tamil	S. India, Sri Lanka Malaysia, Singapore Fiji, Mauritius, Trinidad, Guyana Zanzibar
Telugu	S. E. India
Austronesian	
Tagalog (Philippino)	Philippines
Visayan	Philippines
Indonesian (Bahasa)	Indonesia
Javanese	Java
Malay	Malaya, Thailand, Singapore
Mon Khmer/South East Asian	
Khmer	Cambodia
Mon	Cambodia
Palaung	Burma
Bahnar	Vietnam

We now know that all the languages shaded ▨ on the World Language Family Map belong to the Indo-European language family. Detective work was done by people who study languages (*linguists*) to find this out. They looked at certain words and at what they mean in several languages. They discovered that there are many words with marked similarities across different languages. The similarities between these words show that they are relatives just as you and your brothers and sisters may look a bit like each other, and perhaps like your parents. This degree of similarity in a large number of words leads one to conclude that the languages must have 'grown out' of each other.

H To understand the kind of detective work linguists have done to trace language family trees, look at the following table. You will find words from five languages. The first four languages all belong to the same language family (the Indo-European) but the fifth does not. Read through the words for 'mother' 'brother', and 'water', in the five languages and see if you can see the likeness in the English, German, Czech and Danish words. Now see how different the words are in Hebrew, which is in a different family.

English	German	Czech	Danish	Hebrew
Mother	Mutter	Majka	Mor	Ima
Brother	Bruder	Bratr	Bror	Ach
Water	Wasser	Voda	Vand	Mayim

The words in the languages of the Indo-European family are very similar. Linguists knew that many of the words used in European languages today came from Latin and Greek. It was then discovered that some words were used much earlier in Sanskrit. This is a very old language, now only spoken in prayer and when reading certain texts. Latin, Ancient Greek and Sanskrit are called **classical languages**. This means that nowadays they are read but no longer used in conversation. Sanskrit is the oldest of these three classical languages and the texts which have survived belong to the classical literature of the Hindu religion. It is almost 3,000 years old. Compare the Latin and Ancient Greek with the Sanskrit in this list.

Sanskrit	Latin	Greek	English
dama	domus	domos	house (domestic)
apas	opus	—	work (operation)
nakt	nox	nux	night (equinox)
nasa	nasum	—	nose (nasal)
dvan	duo	duo	two (dual)
trayas	tres	treis	three (tricycle)

Languages travel and change and, over the centuries, create new languages. Sometimes it is not whole languages which travel and change but single words. This may happen when new things are brought to a country from a foreign land. Often the name of the new object travels with it. When this happens, a new word is not invented but the foreign word is adapted or used in its original form by the host language. It may quickly become part of the host language so that its foreign origins are no longer obvious. The language which first gave the meaning to the word can be found in some dictionaries. These are called *etymological* dictionaries. The *etymology* of a word gives us its origin – where it came from in the first place.

Sometimes a word may travel very far, when the thing it names makes a long journey, through many different lands. A famous example of just such a 'wander word' is the English word 'ginger'. Ginger is the name of a plant first grown in central India. (The preserved root of this plant is used in cooking.) Ginger was first taken from India northwards to Persia, then to the Arabian Peninsular and on to the Eastern Mediterranean. It took many years for the plant to reach these places, but when it did, people then introduced it to their neighbouring settlements and countries. So gradually, over many years, the use of ginger root spread right across Eastern and Western Europe, and to Sweden and Finland in the far north.

We know that this is the path by which ginger arrived in Sweden and Finland precisely because we know the words for ginger in the languages of the countries through which the plant made its journey. We also know that the journey lasted hundreds of years because we have some idea of when the word was adopted by the different languages of the countries on the plant's travels. Follow the journey on the map from its beginnings in central India, to its arrival in the far north, in Finland.

These are the modern names for ginger in the languages of the countries through which it travelled. Read them out and see how alike they are.

Middle Indian (Parent language, no longer spoken) – *singivera*

Persian	– *zanjabil*	**Rumanian**	– *ghimber*
Swahili	– *tangawizi*	**Hungarian**	– *gyomber*
Arabic	– *zanjabil*	**French**	– *gingembre*
Hebrew	– *zenghebhil*	**Polish**	– *imbier*
Greek	– *zingiberis*	**German**	– *ingwer*
Georgian	– *janjapili*	**Dutch**	– *gember*
Turkish	– *zencefil*	**English**	– *ginger*
Albanian	– *zenxhefill*	**Irish**	– *gingsear*
Italian	– *zenzero*	**Russian**	– *inbir*
Spanish	– *jengibre*	**Swedish**	– *ingefara*
Portuguese	– *gengivre*	**Finnish**	– *inkivaari*

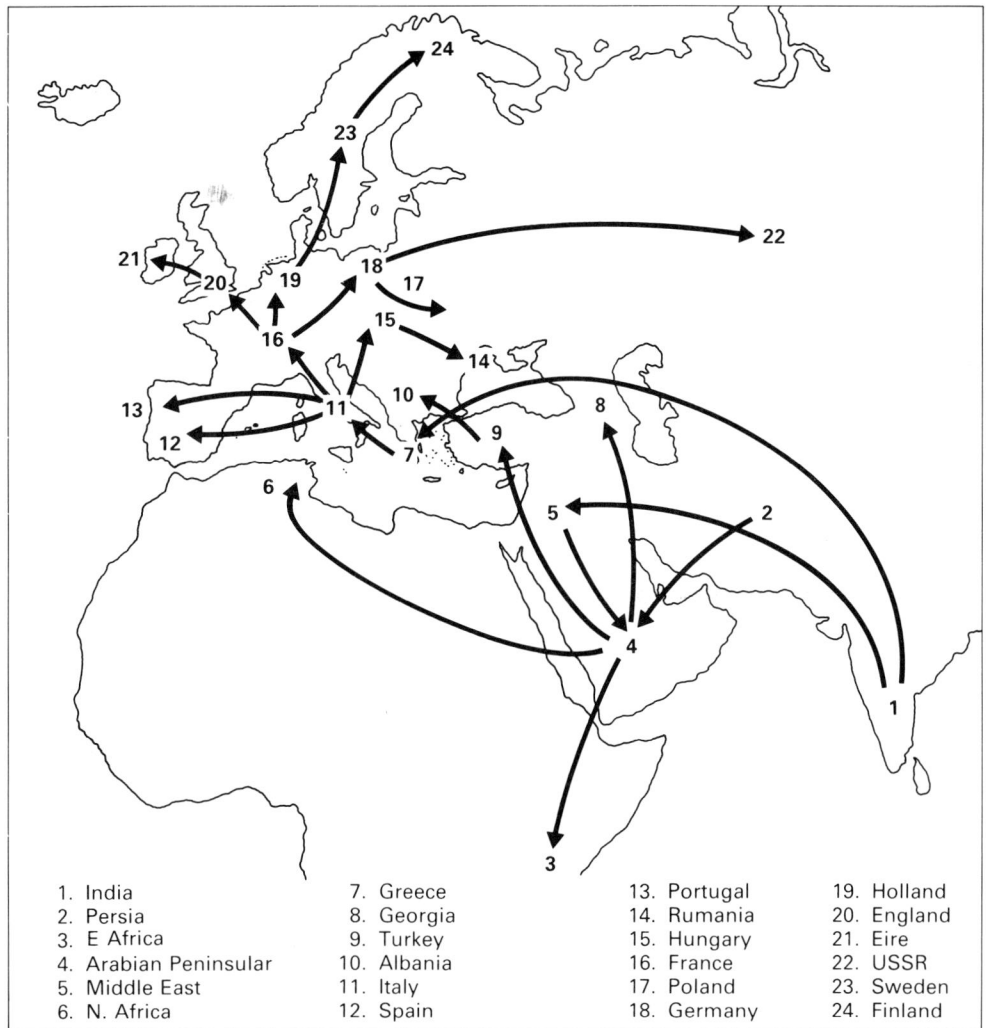

1. India	7. Greece	13. Portugal	19. Holland
2. Persia	8. Georgia	14. Rumania	20. England
3. E Africa	9. Turkey	15. Hungary	21. Eire
4. Arabian Peninsular	10. Albania	16. France	22. USSR
5. Middle East	11. Italy	17. Poland	23. Sweden
6. N. Africa	12. Spain	18. Germany	24. Finland

Another way for words to come into languages is when there is a new invention or discovery. Television, for example, was invented about fifty years ago. Its inventors wanted a name which was based on the classical languages. They chose the word 'television' made up of the ancient Greek word 'tele' which means 'far' and the Latin word 'visum' meaning 'seen'. So the word 'television' actually means 'seen from afar'. Television is an example of an invention which spread all over the world taking its name with it.

1 Look at these examples of the word in five different languages from three different language families.

TELEVISION

	Written	*Spoken*
Tigrinya	ተለቪጅን	television
Arabic	تلفزيون	telefisión
Efik	Television	television
Panjabi	ਟੈਲੀਵਿਜ਼ਨ	television
Russian	ТЕЛЕВИЗОР	tyelyevizor

The words are the same because the invention and the word travelled together. The invention brought its name with it – a new invention, a new word. Compare this to the word for 'food' in these languages. See how different they are. Why do you think this is?

In this unit you have learnt something of the variety of languages spoken in the world today. You may also have found out what languages are spoken by people you know, and where these languages are spoken.

FOOD		
	Written	*Spoken*
Tigrinya	መግቢ	Megbi
Arabic	طعام	Ta'am
Efik	Udia	Udia
Panjabi	ਭੋਜਨ	pojan
Russian	ПИЩА	Pishcha

3 Verbal Communication and Writing Systems

THE DEVELOPMENT OF SPEECH

We communicate a great deal of information through speech. Undoubtedly speech differentiates us from other animals. How and why speech developed in human beings is not known. There is also active scientific debate on the exact nature of the human ability to speak. What is understood is that the human brain is uniquely adapted for speech, and that this occurred some time during the evolutionary process. It is known that '*Homo Erectus*', the earliest human ancestor to stand upright, lived between half a million and one and a half million years ago and it is thought he could probably make many simple sounds. As he is known to have made fire and hunted, it is assumed he may even have used simple words, since these skills require a degree of social organisation. His skull and his brain were smaller than ours although it was larger than those of his earlier ancestors, ape-like creatures called *Hominids* and it has been concluded that these *Hominids* could not talk and did not make fire.

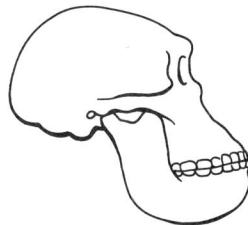

Australopithecus

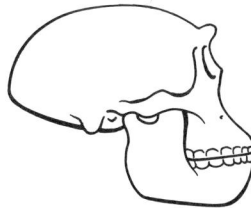

Homo Erectus

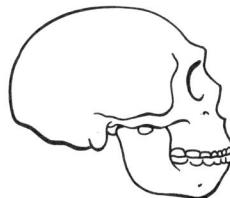

Neanderthal Man

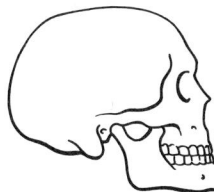

Modern Man

So we do not know exactly when speech began nor how primitive speech was related to animal gestures and sounds. One theory is that speech began after the larynx in the throat had developed in animals which climbed trees. This theory is based on the fact that climbing movements are accompanied by regular exhalations of breath or even interjections, which are short sounds made on exhalations of breath, such as you might make when you are climbing stairs, for example and out of breath. We will see how speech is related to breathing patterns.

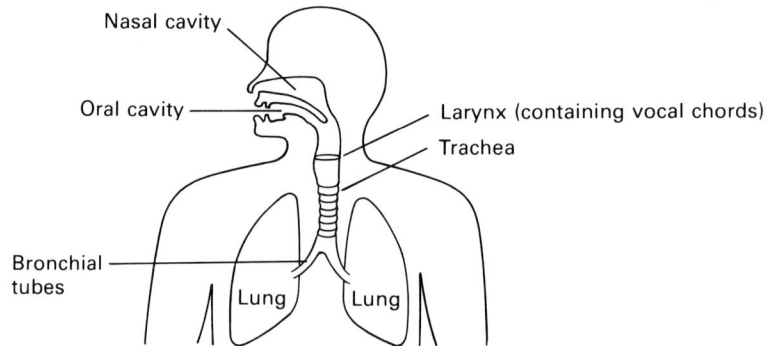

On the diagram find the larynx, which protects the opening to the lungs. After we have taken a breath the air is expelled through the larynx. It passes over our vocal chords, inside the larynx, which then vibrate in the air and produce a sound. This sound is turned into speech by our lips and tongue, which are extremely important in differentiating sounds, as is the way we exhale air through our mouth or nose. To make words we need to shape and form the sound.

Sounds that are made with the mouth completely open are called *vowel* sounds. Sounds that are made by stopping the air flow in some way, with our tongue or lips, are called *consonants*.

A Work on the sound exercises a and b on the tape. Try to imitate exactly what you hear.

B Look up *Phonetics* and *The International Phonetic Alphabet* in a reference book. Write a short piece on why this alphabet may be useful to linguists.

---

fɜ:ˈnetɪks   ˈlaŋwɪdʒ
lɪŋˈwɪstɪks   spiːtʃ

International phonetic script

Most animals need to pick up their food with their mouths. The fact that *Homo sapiens* did not need to do this, because they had a hand with a thumb, left the mouth free to develop into the more complicated structure necessary for speech.

Though no one knows for sure *when* speech developed we know that human beings were able to speak hundreds of thousands of years before they had developed ways of writing language down.

LANGUAGE SKILLS

Today when we learn languages we often talk about there being four skills: only two of these deal with speech.

Speaking   **Listening**   **Writing**   **Reading**

We not only use these language skills when we learn a new language but, of course, we use them every day in our own mother tongue without really thinking about them.

C Think about these four skills now. Which do you use most often and which least? Which one do you think involves you in the most effort? When you were little, in what order did you begin to use them?

You probably decided that *writing* was the last skill you learnt and that it takes more effort than the others. After all, we abandon even a quick note for the milkman, if he arrives at the door and instead we just ask for 'Three pints and six eggs'! Most people decide that they spend least time writing even though there may be some days in school when it doesn't seem like it!

Here is the kind of list that an adult might make on an ordinary day of some of the reading and writing he or she did:

Writing: – wrote a shopping list
             – wrote a cheque for the shopping
             – wrote a letter to a friend
             – wrote a note for my son telling him to put on the supper at 6.30 pm.

Reading: – checked the shopping bill
             – read the newspaper
             – read the television programmes
             – read the instructions on a cakemix
             – looked up a telephone number
             – read a book while having my lunch
             – read a map to plan my journey
             – read the road signs as I drove along

You probably think that this list is quite short and of course if you were a journalist, a writer or an accountant the list would look a bit different.

D As a student, what is your list like? Compile a list of the reading and writing you did yesterday. You need not write down every single piece you did in school but try to give an example of different kinds. For example, writing an essay is not the same as taking notes.

Although we know that our ancestors had been speaking for many thousands of years before writing was invented, today it is hard to imagine a world without writing. It would be a very different world and without written numbers we would also have to do without any technology needing calculations and instructions; there would consequently be no radio or television, no cars or aeroplanes.

E Imagine what would happen in these situations if writing had not been invented:

1 There was a fire in Farmer John's hayrick last week that threatened to burn his barn down. He lives in a village over twenty miles away. There aren't any newspapers so how do you find out about the fire?

2 You have to tell the baker who calls once a week that you want three big loaves of bread. You also have to be at the fair all day and nobody in your family is going to be in and nor are your neighbours. What are you going to do?

3 It is the middle of the winter; it gets dark at 3.30 pm and everybody is bored and feels like 'curling up with a good story'. What do you do instead?

4 Your parents have given you five chickens to look after and say you can keep a profit on all the eggs you sell, if you pay for feeding them. You only have to buy a sack of meal every month but you sell the eggs every day. How do you work out how much money you have made?

5 You hear that there is a good job going in the nearby town and want to 'apply' for it. How do you set about it?

If we look closely at the lists we made and at the situations you have just solved, we can see that writing is used in different ways and for different reasons.

- it helps us *remember* things, as when we write a shopping list or take notes at school.
- we use it to *communicate* information, as when we write messages, letters or read a newspaper.
- it is used in *business*, when we write a bill, or a cheque or keep a *record* of the number of eggs sold!

Before Writing

Our ancestors had already been drawing pictures of the living world for many thousands of years before writing was invented. Cave paintings of the animals hunted by early man have been found dating back to approximately 20,000 years BC.

Almost certainly these paintings were not just decorative but were connected with magic or religion and many people believe that some of them are *recording* events.

There are societies which have a simplified system of keeping records through using objects. For example, the North American Indians use strings of different coloured beads often tied together to form a belt which is called a *wampum*. White beads denote 'peace' and purple

Wampum

beads denote 'war'. The numbers and patterns used form a simple record of events.

The *Cara* tribes of Ecuador keep records by putting pebbles of different colours, shapes and sizes into small boxes. However, while these 'object writing' systems can be used to keep records, none of them can tell a story.

Cave paintings from Lascaux, South-West France

Pictograms

The earliest writing developed from 'pictures' which could be put together to form a narrative. We call these 'pictures' *pictograms* (a word made up of *pingere* = to paint (Latin) and *gramma* = written (Greek)). Pictograms are symbols which always convey the same messages. For example, early man might have drawn himself like this:

To portray a hunter he could add a spear. As a result, the pictogram for hunter would look like this:

Early on he might have drawn three men like this:

but quite soon he would want to simplify and speed up his system, perhaps by putting scratches to indicate the number.

F Draw your own pictogram for five hunters and then look at these modern pictograms. What do they mean? Would they be understood by a visitor to England from Russia or Thailand?

 a

 b

 c

 d

 e

 f

Can you think of or find another six pictograms? Would they all be understood by foreign visitors?

Pictograms are still used all over the world to give information in public places because they are easily understood. Nearly all our road signs are pictograms. They can be read very quickly even while driving and understood by everyone.

G We are going to look at what makes a good pictogram. Draw pictograms for the six objects listed below in muddled order and make up three of your own as well. When you are happy with your nine pictograms swap with a friend and try to understand each other's drawings. Remember you must not write anything, not even numbers.

a cake   a teacher   a car   an aeroplane   a shark   money

Were they all easy to recognise? The first six were probably not too difficult but how about the 'unknown' ones? Now redraw any that were not clear and see if you can draw all of them a bit faster even if you have to leave out some details.

Here is an example of what might happen in the development of 'fish' from:

picture   pictogram

As our writer was trying to write faster and faster he oversimplified and drew some fish that were not really recognisable. So he had to go back to an earlier stage and put the eye back in to make his fish clear.

Can you suggest some rules for drawing successful pictograms?

Ideograms

A great many things we want to tell each other about are not objects you can see or feel, but actions, ideas, and feelings. Abstract feelings or notions are much more difficult to draw. Here is our first hunter again:

If the spear he is carrying for the hunt is also used to fight against other groups of people our writer might decide to show the idea of 'war' by drawing a spear:

and later a broken spear might show the idea of 'peace'.

These are 'idea pictures' or *ideograms*.
In Chinese, the pictogram of a pig is used to show several different ideas. First the animal itself:

Then 'roof'

over 'pig' gives the ideogram for 'family'.

To understand why, we have to realise that for thousands of years the Chinese have kept domestic pigs which are felt to have close ties with the home and family.

By combining 'woman',

'roof' and 'pig' the Chinese make an ideogram

which means 'to marry'. The woman adds to her possessions a home and family. The humble domesticated pig is still in there!

H Now try making up your own ideograms for:
1 Don't drink and drive.
2 To speak.
3 Quickly.
4 Angry.
The last two are quite difficult, aren't they?

This is how the Chinese write angry: 嬲

It is made up of 'man' twice 男 男

with a *character* you already know showing that two men fighting over the same woman is likely to make somebody very angry!

CHINA: LAND, LANGUAGE AND PEOPLE

The Peoples' Republic of China covers an area of over 10,000,000 square kilometres.

It has enormous variations of landscape and climate. The people come from different racial groups, look very different, have different ways of life and speak many different varieties of Chinese.

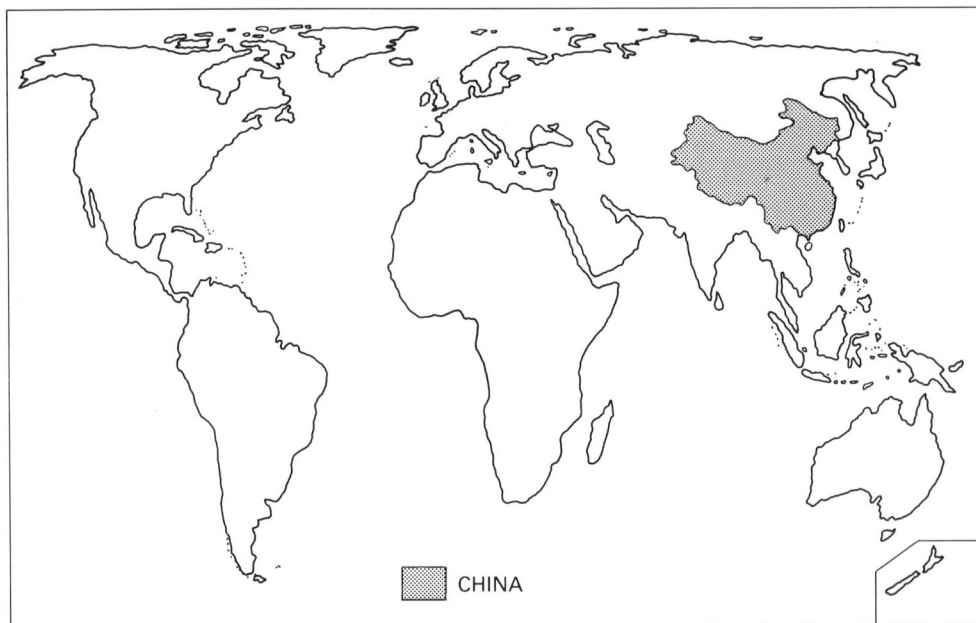

CHINA

We already know that more people speak Chinese than any other language: at least 1,000 million in the Peoples' Republic of China alone. Chinese is also spoken in other countries: Taiwan, Hong Kong, Thailand, Malaysia, Singapore and wherever the Chinese people have settled.

Uighi citizen, Sinkiang

Mother and child, Deprung, Tibet

Pekingese man, with Mongol features

Hakka peasant, Hong Kong

Qiang woman, Maoewn

About two-thirds of the population of the Peoples' Republic speak *Mandarin* which is considered the standard language but even Mandarin varies a lot from region to region. Then there is *Wu* from the Shanghai region, *Cantonese* from the South and *Min*, *Hakka*, *Hsiang* and other varieties spoken by a smaller percentage of the population. A person living in the South, in Canton province and speaking Cantonese will probably not be able to understand a person from Szechwan in Central China and is even less likely to understand the languages spoken in the northern and western provinces.

Map labels:

KAZAKH

UIGHUR

MONGOL

NORTHERN MANDARIN

TIBETAN

MANCHU

HSIANG

WU

MIAO

SOUTHERN MANDARIN

FUKIENESE

YI

CHUANG

HAKKA

CANTONESE

Chinese languages

Chinese Writing

In approximately 215 BC the Emperor Chin Shik Huang Ti began building the Great Wall of China to keep out the tribes from the north. He sacrificed many thousands of people working in terrible conditions building the Great Wall.

He burned the books of the great thinker Confucius and buried scholars alive. However, because he unified the written form of the language, people who cannot understand each other face to face as a result of the differences in their spoken languages can write to each other with ease. So the cruel Emperor Chin Shik Huang Ti has a lasting monument in modern China in every open book, poster on the main road, or letter from a friend.

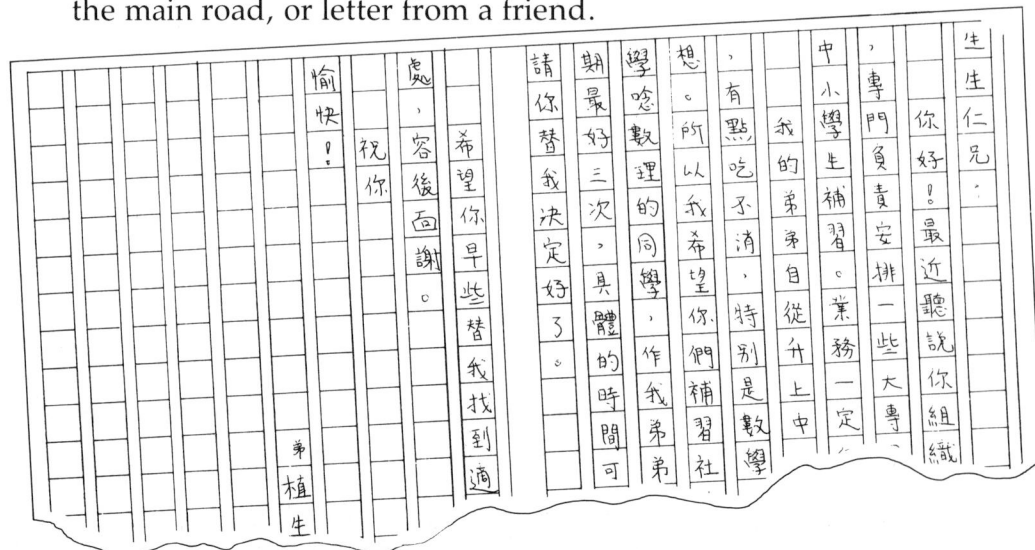

We have already looked at a few Chinese ideograms but Chinese is written with many thousands. They are called *characters*. A large dictionary might have as many as 50,000, a Chinese type-writer might have up to 5,400 and if you were at Primary school in Hong Kong you would probably have to spend at least an hour every night just on writing practice. You need to know at least 3,500 characters to do secondary school work.

The earliest Chinese writing found was drawn on the shoulder-bones of large animals. These were simple pictograms. The legendary inventor of the first Chinese writing, Ts'ang Chienh, is said to have worked out his simple images by studying nature.

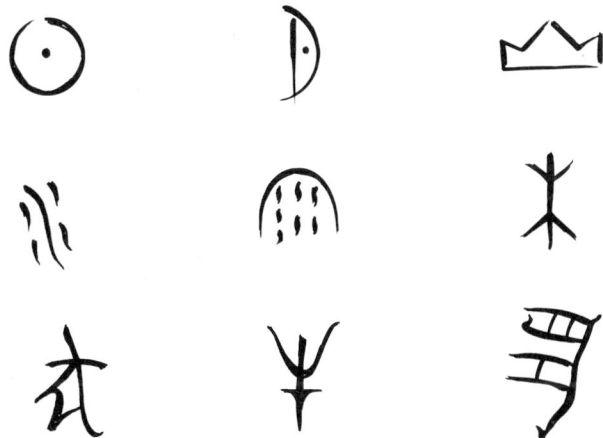

Nine Chinese pictograms

Look at Ts'ang Chienh's pictograms and see if you can decide what each one stands for. Here are the meanings in muddled order:

water rain wood moon cattle sun mountain horse dog

Were they easy to work out?

The same nine pictograms from original to modern form

You will find the same pictograms on the left. The middle and right-hand columns show how the original images have developed right up to the present day. The right-hand column shows *Chen Shu* or regular style which is still used today in Hong Kong and Taiwan. 'Regular' here means the original way of writing.

In 1955 in the Peoples' Republic a simplified system was introduced which is now taught in schools all over mainland China. Not all characters can be simplified. Here are some examples of Chinese written in both forms.

Regular   **Simplified**

龍   龙

Dragon

雲   云

Cloud

飛   飞

Fly

開   开

Open

葉   叶

Leaf

手
人

Hand
People } cannot be simplified

Regular and simplified systems

From writing on bone, to engraving on bronze the Chinese moved to the brush which has been used for many centuries. There are still Chinese *calligraphers* or expert writers who use a brush. Because the brush is flexible you can see differences in the width of the strokes.

The traditional direction of Chinese writing was from top to bottom vertically down the page starting on the right. However the direction does not matter very much in Chinese and it is now more usual to write across the page horizontally from left to right. Of course, most students use a ball-point pen nowadays!

K You can use your ball-point to practise writing some Chinese but you could also try a thick felt-tip pen with a chisel edge. It makes a good substitute for a brush and you can get a better idea of the thick and thin strokes. Copy the characters below several times until you feel confident, starting with the strokes in the top left-hand corner of each character. Try to keep them the same size or use some centimetre squared paper. This is how primary school children start learning to write in Hong Kong.

看見	樹林	他們	木
see	forest	they	wood

我	他	書	黑
I	he	book	black

筆	羊	魚	飯
pen	sheep	fish	rice

買	煮	和	她
buy	cook	and	she

嗎	在	白	大	不
forms a question	in	white	big	not

Note that the Chinese need two characters for 'they'. Can you recognise the first one? Many words have two characters. Look at 'see' and 'forest'. Notice how the second character for 'forest' is made up of two of the signs for 'tree'.

L Now that you are familiar with the characters you can start reading Chinese. Read the sentences below without looking back. They are written vertically and are numbered in Chinese.

43

五．他們看見黑羊嗎？

四．我不買書和筆。

三．他們看見大樹林。

二．她看見白羊。

一．他煮飯。

You probably noticed that there was *no* need to change fish**es** *nor* to add an **s** to he cook**s**. Chinese is a very complex language to write so it is lucky that there are a few things we don't have to worry about!

M You can now write some sentences of your own. You probably feel quite confident about some of the characters already. Look back at the more complicated ones if you need to and remember to try to keep them the same size. You can choose the direction in which to write your sentences but remember to number them in Chinese, with a full-stop after the number.

1 I cook rice.
2 He cooks large fishes and rice.
3 They buy large books.
4 Does he buy pens and black books?
5 I do not buy fish.
6 They, in the woods, do not see white sheep.

Notice that although we can understand sentence 6, the word order sounds a bit odd to us. We would be more likely to say 'They don't see any white sheep in the woods' but you must write the Chinese in the above order to get it right. Now make up some sentences of your own and swap them with a friend. Read the English back to each other.

Writing materials

We have seen how the use of brush and ink influenced the form of Chinese writing. We know the ancient civilisations like the Sumerians, the Egyptians, the Hittites as well as the Chinese had different kinds of picture writing and the materials used often influenced the form.

(N) Make a list of as many tools for writing and surfaces to write on as you can think of.

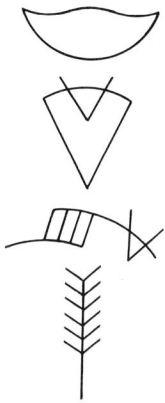

The Sumerians who lived on the Persian Gulf lived in an area with few trees or rocks, so they used damp clay from the river bed and made marks on it with the reeds growing nearby. They then baked the clay to make a hard tablet so that they could keep their records. In the beginning they made both curved and straight lines and wrote vertically down the clay.

They then started to write from left to right to avoid smudging the wet clay and turned their pictograms round.

They also found that the wedge-shaped or *cuneiform* shape of the reeds they were using made it much easier to draw straight lines. As a result, their writing became completely straight, as you can see from the chart below.

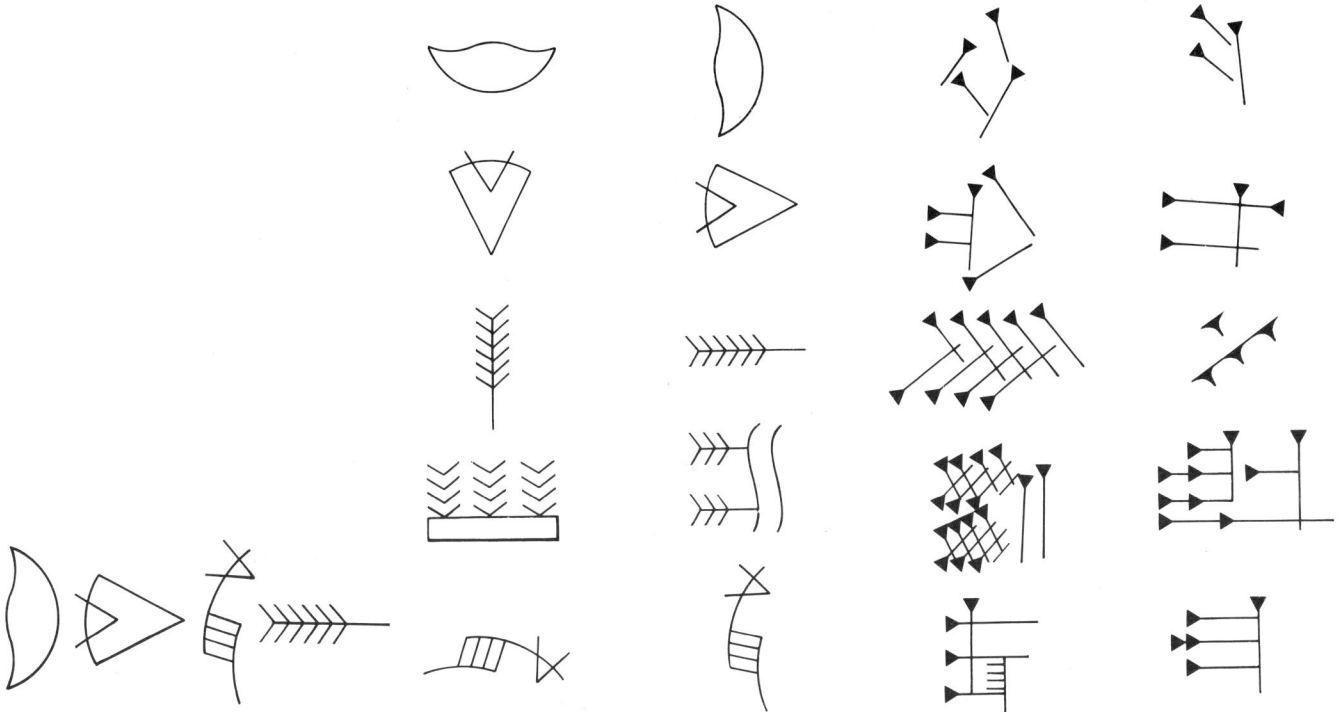

Vertical cuneiform writing

Horizontal cuneiform writing

Section of cuneiform writing

45

O Copy out the chart and write the meanings of the symbols beside each. You could try making a plasticene 'tablet' and use a wedge shaped stick to really get the feel of cuneiform writing. In muddled order they are:

orchard	grain	to plough	ox	sun

Hieroglyphs

About 5,000 years ago the Egyptians developed a *pictograph* writing system that was carved or painted on stone by priests. They thought of the thousands of stylised picture symbols as the 'words of the gods'. We call their writing *hieroglyphics* which is the Greek way of saying 'sacred carvings'.

Here is the name of a famous Egyptian queen. It has the ring drawn around it for divine protection like all royal names in Egypt.

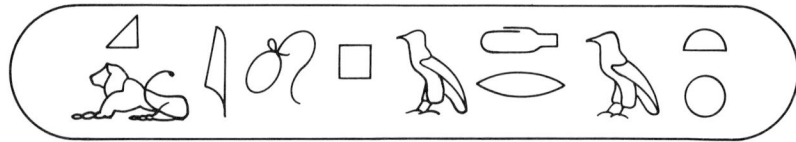

Cleopatra

The Egyptians carved their *hieroglyphs* into both wood and stone and also wrote on a paper made from the 'papyrus', a tall reed which grew in the swamps. With this paper they used a reed 'brush' and ink.

Papyrus reeds

A page from the Great Harris Papyrus with hieroglyphics, showing Pharaoh Rameses IV addressing three gods

Papyrus, written in hieroglyphics

The *Egyptian hieroglyphic* system was only used for religious writings and recording royal events. Two other forms of writing developed very early and were used at the same time as the hieroglyphs:

Hieratic script: a section from the
Great Harris Papyrus showing a list of
all the donations made by the
Egyptian people to the temple,
recorded in the reign of Rameses IV,
c.1160 BC

hieratic

Demotic script: a section from *The
Instructions of Onkhsheshonqy*, a
wisdom text, c. 100 BC

and *demotic*.

Hieratic was a simplified sort of 'shorthand' used by priests and scribes and *demotic* was used in business, in government decrees and for social writing. We can see that these scripts, which were never carved in stone look very different from the hieroglyphs.

The hieroglyphic system was extremely complicated because some of the symbols were real pictograms or ideograms representing objects. For example, see below the hieroglyphic for 'mu' meaning water.

The Egyptians also used symbols to stand for *syllables* and sometimes they stood for *single sounds*. In some inscriptions 'mu' is written not as above but with two pictograms giving the *sound* 'mu'.

m + u

Because the Egyptians used these different systems mixed together it has been very difficult to *decipher* their writing and they never developed a complete *alphabet*.

P We can try making up an *alphabet* of *phonograms* (pictures standing for sounds. You will find several sentences below to start you off.

47

Alphabets

Archaeologists and linguists believe that the first real *alphabet* or system of signs representing sounds was probably invented by the Phoenicians who lived on the eastern Mediterranean. They spoke a *semitic* language, from the same family as *Hebrew* and *Arabic,* and did not need to use written vowels at all times.

The Phoenicians were very skilled sailors and traded throughout the Mediterranean, with the result that their writing system was adopted by the people who came into contact with them.

When they began to trade with the Phoenicians the Greeks, who had no writing system, adopted Phoenician letters and based their alphabet on them. They invented characters for vowels to make writing easier and got rid of any Phoenician letters representing sounds that the Greek language did not use. They still did not leave spaces between words or use any punctuation, however.

Hieroglyph	Phoenician	Greek 500 BC	Roman
		A *alpha*	**A**
		B *beta*	**B**

Progression from hieroglyphics to the Roman alphabet

From the Greeks, the system passed via the Etruscans in Italy to the Romans who simplified the Greek alphabet still further. In turn, as the Romans expanded their Empire, their writing spread throughout Europe. English is written in the *Roman alphabet* or *Latin script*. It looks just like Latin but is quite different from modern Greek, although you can see the family resemblance.

Τρία κόκκινα περιστέρια μέσα στὸ φῶς χαράζοντας τὴ μοίρα μας μέσα στὸ φῶς μὲ χρώματα καὶ χειρονομίες ἀνθρώπων ποὺ ἀγαπήσαμε.

musca —ae, f.

musca domestica insectum est e genere dipterorum
muscarium est *flabellum*, quo muscae molestae abiguntur.

Three red pigeons in the light inscribing our fate in the light with colors and gestures of people we have loved.

Scripts of the World

There are many different scripts in use today but not nearly as many as there are languages; consequently, when we learn a new language we do not always have to learn a new script. The Latin script is not the only one to have been widely adopted.

Q Using the map of script families to help you, make a list of all the languages you can think of which use the Latin script.

Why does much of Africa also use the Latin script? Why is the whole of North and South America included in this script area?

Latin is only one of several very successful world scripts. The map shows us that scripts like Arabic, Cyrillic, Devanagari and its variations and the Chinese characters we have already studied are also used over wide areas and by very many people.

Now look at the chart which shows how the script invented by the Phoenicians was the basis for the writing systems of several 'families' of related scripts.

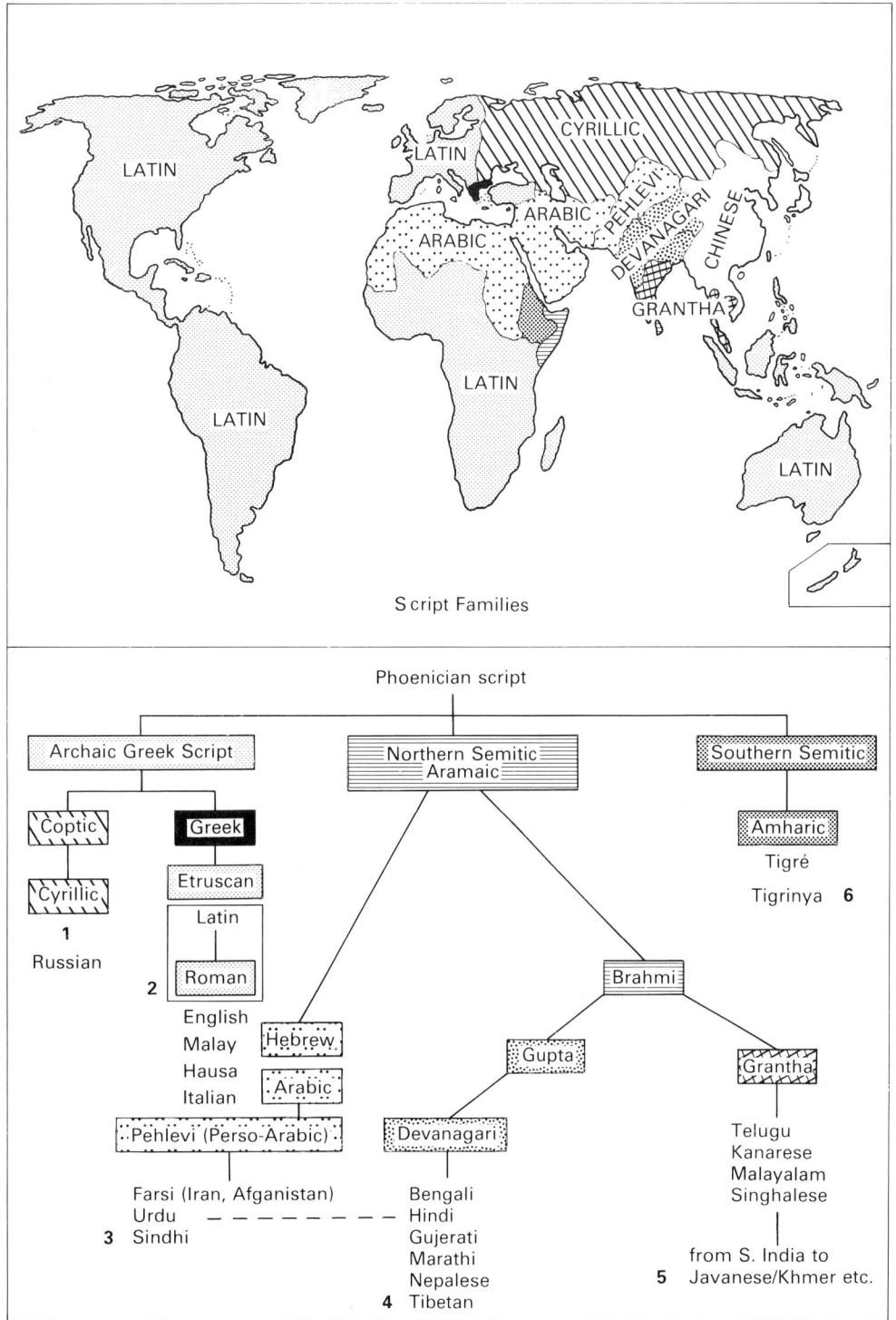

Script Families

Phoenician script

| Archaic Greek Script | Northern Semitic Aramaic | Southern Semitic |

Coptic — Greek

Cyrillic — Etruscan
1 — Latin
Russian — Roman
2

English
Malay — Hebrew
Hausa
Italian — Arabic

Pehlevi (Perso-Arabic)

Farsi (Iran, Afganistan)
Urdu — — — — — — — —
3 Sindhi

Amharic
Tigré
Tigrinya 6

Brahmi

Gupta — Grantha

Devanagari

Bengali
Hindi
Gujerati
Marathi
Nepalese
4 Tibetan

Telugu
Kanarese
Malayalam
Singhalese

from S. India to
5 Javanese/Khmer etc.

R Look carefully at the examples of each 'family' of scripts and check on the world map where they are used.

The Chinese and Japanese languages are very different. In fact no definite link is recognised between Japanese and *any other language in the world*. The Japanese adopted Chinese characters in the third century AD and simplified them.

垂　氷　　　　　　　　　　　百　穂

窓にうつる　垂氷の影の　一ならび

今宵の月夜　あきらけくこそ

Icicles　　　　　　　　　　Hyakusui

A row of icicles

　　Against the window glitters bright ;

Undoubtedly the moon

　　Is shining brilliantly to-night.

Japanese script

Does this mean we could use Chinese characters to write English? Could Latin script be used to write Chinese?

S Try to make a collection of as many different scripts as you can. You may have friends who can write in another script, or have notices in your school or shop signs in your town to give you ideas. Try to find some newspapers or books in the library using other scripts.

4 Semitic Languages

ARABIC

These are the countries where Arabic is the national language:

Country	Population (Million)	Capital
Egypt	50	Cairo
Algeria	23	Algiers
Mauritania	2	Nouakchott
Morocco	22	Rabat
Tunisia	7	Tunis
Sudan	20	Khartoum
Libya	4	Tripoli
Jordan	3	Amman
Lebanon	3	Beirut
Syria	10	Damascus
Iraq	15	Baghdad
Saudi Arabia	10	Riyadh
Oman	1.8	Muscat
Yemen Arab Republic	8	San'a
People's Democratic Republic of Yemen	2.5	Aden
Kuwait	1.8	Kuwait
United Arab Emirates	1.4	Abu Dhabi (largest city)
Bahrain	0.4	Manama
Qatar	0.3	Doha

The total Arabic speaking population is approximately 170 million.

Significance of Arabic

Political

Arabic is the national language of many oil producing states whose first natural resource has brought these countries, relatively recently, into the arena of international commerce and industry. This has

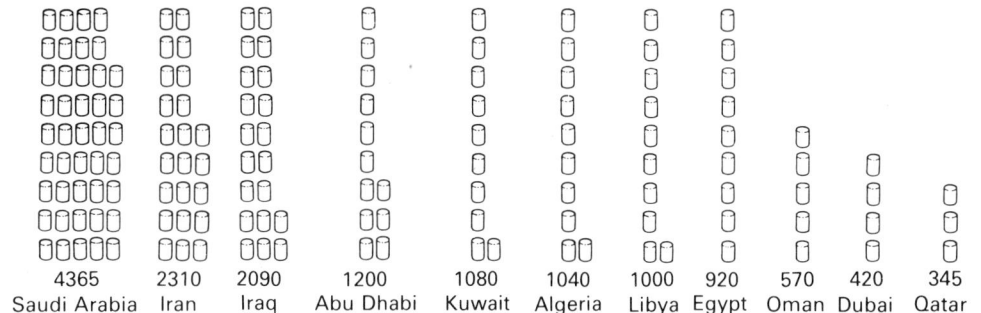

4365	2310	2090	1200	1080	1040	1000	920	570	420	345
Saudi Arabia	Iran	Iraq	Abu Dhabi	Kuwait	Algeria	Libya	Egypt	Oman	Dubai	Qatar

1987 Thousand barrels per day oil production in main oil producing Arab states.
Figures supplied by *British Petroleum Statistical Review 1987*.

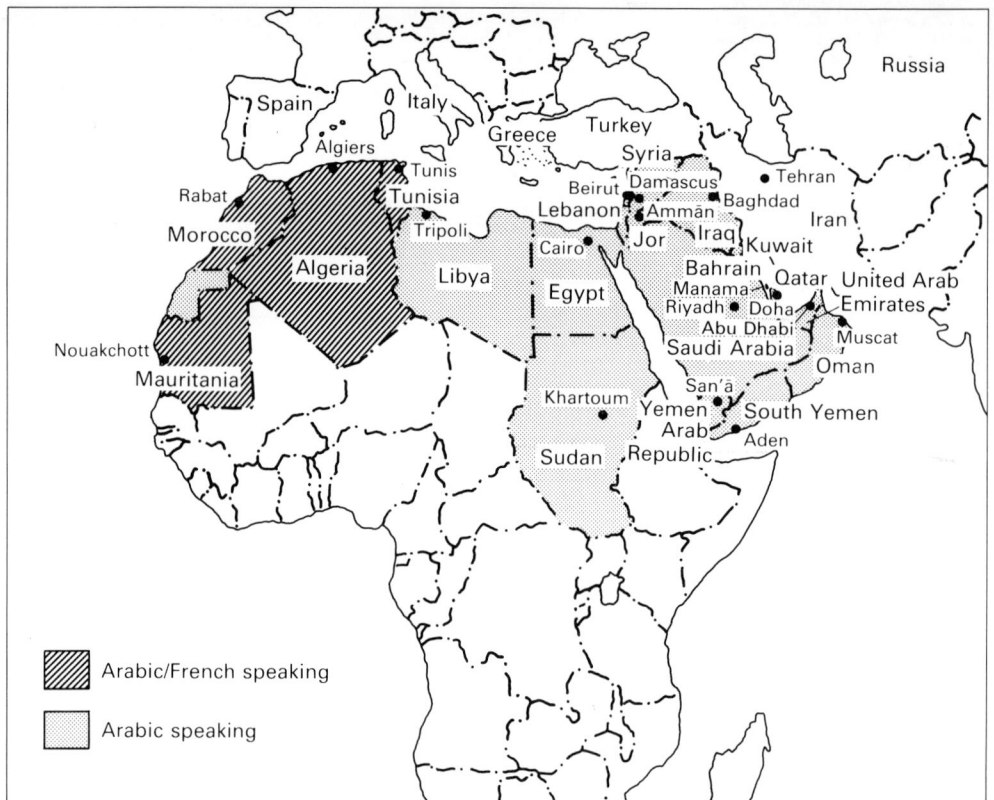

altered the nature of the relationship between these states and the rest of the world. Therefore nowadays Arabic has a world significance not based solely on the number of its speakers.

Religious

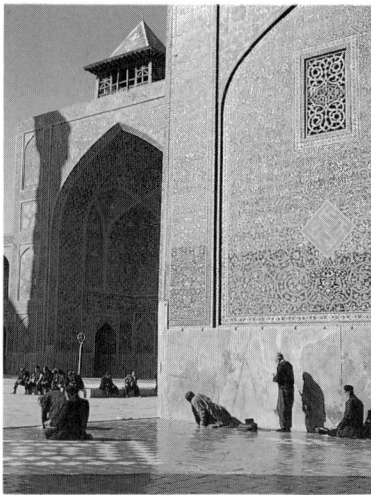

Moslems praying outside the Royal Mosque, Isfahan, Iran

Arabic is a *liturgical* tongue learnt by Islamic peoples throughout the world for study and prayer as the Qu'ran is written in the Arabic dialect of seventh century Mecca. Therefore Arabic is often learnt as the second language in many Islamic countries such as Pakistan, Bangladesh and Iran so that the orthodox may at least pray and read in Classical Arabic.

Islamic countries of the world

All Islamic states, including Turkey, Malaysia and Bangladesh for example, recognise the greeting: *Salaam Alequm*. Though these states are geographically disparate, they share a common link through Islam and Arabic. Each has an entirely different national language (Turkish, Malay, Bengali etc.). However, these and many other national languages (Farsi, Urdu, Hausa and Swahili) share many Arabic influences.

Historical

إذا صح منك الودّ فالكل هين   وكل الذي فوق التراب تراب

Arabic inscription: Rabia Al-Adawiyya (Sufi poet), AD 801

If I secure your love, then all else is insignificant and all on earth is nought but earth.

Arabic is a relatively recent language: no inscription has been found dated earlier than the year 328 AD, though it belongs to the *Semitic* language family (refer to the section on Hebrew). Its use expanded rapidly in the seventh century when it became the voice of the new world religion, Islam. As the prophet Mohammed spoke the dialect of Mecca, the sacred books were naturally written in the Mecca dialect rather than that of Medina, the city to which he fled in September 622. Year one in Muslim chronology is consequently AD 622, but as the Muslim year contains fewer than 365 days we are therefore in the year 1409-10, (1989/1990).

١٤١٠

The year 1410 in Arabic numerals

The Ka'bah, Mecca

It was believed a sacred duty to spread the new religion as widely as possible and within less than a hundred years the Arab Muslims ruled an empire which extended from Spain in the West to the borders with India in the East. Later it was to spread even further east. The rewards of being a faithful Muslim were very attractive and to achieve them, the word was to be spread beyond Arabia; Islam was to conquer the world.

Trading developed with ease and with considerably less danger because goods could now travel over vast areas without encountering an alien frontier. As Arabic travelled with the conquerers, it became the language of trade and the Islamic world shared the common currency of the dinar.

Muslim traders were also responsible for the introduction of paper-making skills and the use of Arabic numerals into the Mediterranean region. From India, Muslim traders learnt a convenient way of recording numbers, using nine digits and a zero, which was to replace the cumbersome Roman system and facilitate addition and subtraction in columns.

The Arabic legacy included the introduction into Europe and especially into Spain, of windmills to grind sugar-cane. In addition, through ingenious methods of irrigation, large areas of barren land were made fertile. Muslims were also responsible for creating important centres of learning which produced translations of many major works of literature and science which thus became available to the Christian world in Latin. The stained glass windows of medieval churches and the many coloured tiles still used in Spain are both imitations of Islamic art. The new products and ideas reaching Europe through the spread of Islam often went on being called by an Arabic name, e.g. sugar, syrup and coffee. In Arabic and Spanish respectively, they are: 'sukkar, azúcar,' 'morrabba, jarabe' and 'kahwah, café'.

Literary Arabic is standardised throughout the entire Arabic world, but there are differences in detail in the colloquial Arabic of different countries. The differences are small compared with the similarities.

Alcazar Palace, Seville

English	Moroccan		Classical Arabic	
why?	alash	عـلاش	limadha	لــاذا
tea	atay	أتـاي	shay	شـاي
O.K. yes	wakha	واخـي	naam	نـعـم
shoe	sabaat	سـبـاط	hidha	حـذاء
mad	mkardel	مخـردل	mjnoon	مجـنـون
sheep	houli	حـولـي	kebsh	كبـش

Arabic, like Hebrew, is characterised by trilateral or triconsonantal roots. For example, *Islam* (meaning 'resignation') is based on the three consonants **s, l** and **m**, as in *Salaam* ('peace') and *Muslim* ('the resigned one'). Notice the word *Shalom* ('peace') in Hebrew also has the consonants **s, l** and **m**. Unit Two on World Languages expands on their close link and when you have completed the speaking exercises in Arabic and moved on to written Hebrew, you will see that the roots of words are the consonants and will learn to recognise the use of vowel points.

خـــادم الحـــرمـــين الشـــريفـــين:
لن أترد د في إتمام أى إنجاز
من أجل مكــة المـكرمـة

مكة المكرمة ـ واس: اعلن خادم الحرمين الشريفين الملك فهد بن عبد العزيز آل سعود ان مشروع توسعة الحرم الشريف ماهو
إلا مقدمة لمشروعات وانجازات اسلامية اخرى. وقال في كلمة ارتجلها قبل ان يقوم بوضع حجر الاساس وازاحة اللوحة التذكارية
لمشروع التوسعة ان شعوره كشعور اي مواطن في هذه البلاد يرى هذا الانجاز العظيم الذي سوف ينتهي في وقت قياسي قريب
قياسا على نوعية البناء التي كانت موجودة في التوسعة الاولى.

An example of Arabic script with points: extract from the daily newspaper Asharq Al-Awsat, 14 September 1988, vol. 11 no. 3578

Vocabulary

A Listen to the tape and learn some useful Arabic phrases. Remember that here we are using the Roman alphabet as a phonetic transcription of the Arabic alphabet.

Ahlan = Hello!
Ahlan ya Paul = Hello Paul!
Qef halak? = How are you? (mas.)
Kwaiss shukran = Well, thank you.
Qef halik? = How are you? (fem.)
Kwaissa shukran = Well, thank you.
She ismak? = What is your name? (mas.)   Ismi Paul.
She ismik? = What is your name? (fem.)   Ismi Anne.
Salaam Alequm = Peace unto you. (pl. mas.)
Waalequm Salaam = Peace unto you too. (said in reply to above)
Maasalaamah = Goodbye.

"Ahlan ya John. Qef halak?"

1	א	6	ו
2	ב	7	ז
3	ג	8	ח
4	ד	9	ט
5	ה	10	י

Numbers

1	wāhed	6	sīta
2	itnēn	7	sābaa
3	telēta	8	temānia
4	ārbaa	9	tīza
5	hāmsa	10	āshara

arbaa saed telata yusawi sabaa: $4 + 3 = 7$

hamsa nakis itnen yusawi telata: $5 - 2 = 3$

Practise some mental arithmetic with your friends in Arabic!

First column: Arabic numerals. Second column: Modern Arabic numerals

HEBREW

Hebrew and Arabic are the principal survivors of the Semitic group of languages. Hebrew has been the language of prayer for Jews throughout their history.

וַיְדַבֵּר אֱלֹהִים אֵת כָּל־הַדְּבָרִים הָאֵלֶּה לֵאמֹר: ס אָנֹכִי
יְהוָה אֱלֹהֶיךָ אֲשֶׁר הוֹצֵאתִיךָ מֵאֶרֶץ מִצְרַיִם מִבֵּית עֲבָדִים:
לֹא־יִהְיֶה לְךָ אֱלֹהִים אֲחֵרִים עַל־פָּנָי: לֹא־תַעֲשֶׂה לְךָ
פֶסֶל ׀ וְכָל־תְּמוּנָה אֲשֶׁר בַּשָּׁמַיִם ׀ מִמַּעַל וַאֲשֶׁר בָּאָרֶץ
מִתַּחַת וַאֲשֶׁר בַּמַּיִם ׀ מִתַּחַת לָאָרֶץ: לֹא־תִשְׁתַּחֲוֶה לָהֶם
וְלֹא תָעָבְדֵם כִּי אָנֹכִי יְהוָה אֱלֹהֶיךָ אֵל קַנָּא פֹּקֵד עֲוֺן
אָבֹת עַל־בָּנִים עַל־שִׁלֵּשִׁים וְעַל־רִבֵּעִים לְשֹׂנְאָי: וְעֹשֶׂה
חֶסֶד לַאֲלָפִים לְאֹהֲבַי וּלְשֹׁמְרֵי מִצְוֺתָי: ס   לֹא תִשָּׂא
אֶת־שֵׁם־יְהוָה אֱלֹהֶיךָ לַשָּׁוְא כִּי לֹא יְנַקֶּה יְהוָה אֵת אֲשֶׁר־
יִשָּׂא אֶת־שְׁמוֹ לַשָּׁוְא:
פ

זָכוֹר אֶת־יוֹם הַשַּׁבָּת לְקַדְּשׁוֹ: שֵׁשֶׁת יָמִים תַּעֲבֹד וְעָשִׂיתָ
כָּל־מְלַאכְתֶּךָ: וְיוֹם הַשְּׁבִיעִי שַׁבָּת ׀ לַיהוָה אֱלֹהֶיךָ לֹא־
תַעֲשֶׂה כָל־מְלָאכָה אַתָּה ׀ וּבִנְךָ־וּבִתֶּךָ עַבְדְּךָ וַאֲמָתְךָ
וּבְהֶמְתֶּךָ וְגֵרְךָ אֲשֶׁר בִּשְׁעָרֶיךָ: כִּי שֵׁשֶׁת־יָמִים עָשָׂה
יְהוָה אֶת־הַשָּׁמַיִם וְאֶת־הָאָרֶץ אֶת־הַיָּם וְאֶת־כָּל־אֲשֶׁר־בָּם
וַיָּנַח בַּיּוֹם הַשְּׁבִיעִי עַל־כֵּן בֵּרַךְ יְהוָה אֶת־יוֹם הַשַּׁבָּת
וַיְקַדְּשֵׁהוּ:   ס   כַּבֵּד אֶת־אָבִיךָ וְאֶת־אִמֶּךָ לְמַעַן יַאֲרִכוּן
יָמֶיךָ עַל הָאֲדָמָה אֲשֶׁר־יְהוָה אֱלֹהֶיךָ נֹתֵן לָךְ:   ס   לֹא
תִּרְצָח: ס   לֹא תִּנְאָף: ס   לֹא תִּגְנֹב: ס   לֹא־
תַעֲנֶה בְרֵעֲךָ עֵד שָׁקֶר: ס   לֹא תַחְמֹד בֵּית רֵעֶךָ
ס   לֹא תַחְמֹד אֵשֶׁת רֵעֶךָ וְעַבְדּוֹ וַאֲמָתוֹ וְשׁוֹרוֹ וַחֲמֹרוֹ
וְכֹל אֲשֶׁר לְרֵעֶךָ:
פ

Dacalogue panel (Ten Commandments), Falmouth Synagogue, c. 1800

The Ten Commandments in Hebrew

Modern Hebrew is now spoken in Israel and learnt as a language by many Jews in the Diaspora, the areas of Jewish settlement outside Israel. Hebrew has a very high number of *cognates* (related words) with Arabic.

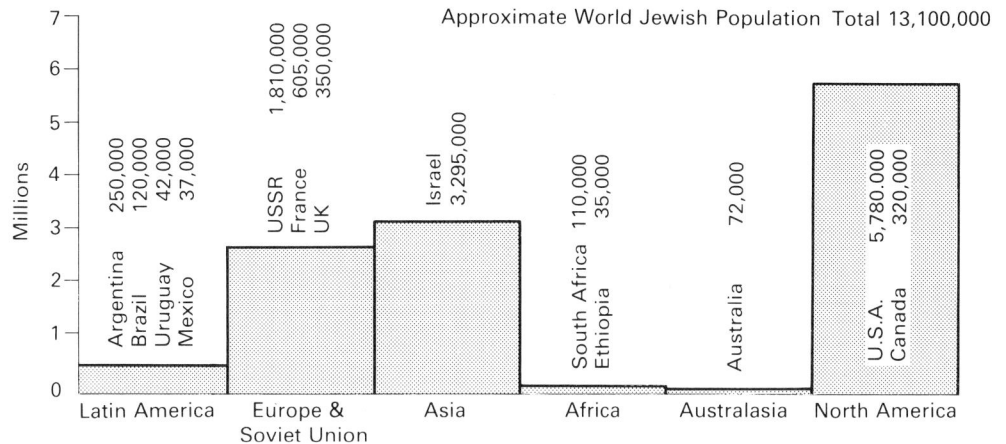

Approximate World Jewish Population Total 13,100,000

You are now going to look at Hebrew as a writing and reading system and learn how to read with ease. Hebrew, like Arabic, is read from right to left ◄——— and its alphabet has been used to write other languages. *Yiddish*, the language of Eastern European Jews, is very similar to German and is written in the Hebrew alphabet. *Ladino* is an old form of Spanish, spoken to this day by the descendants of Jews who left Spain because of the Spanish Inquisition in 1492. It can also be written in the Hebrew script.

Below you will see two different scripts. The first is standard Hebrew script, whilst the second, *Ladino*, is written in the *Rabbinic* script. There is a third script used for everyday written communications and for school work.

בבהילו יצאנו ממצרים **1**

הָא לַחְמָא עַנְיָא דִּי אֲכָלוּ אַבְהָתָנָא בְּאַרְעָא דְמִצְרָיִם. כָּל **2**
דִּכְפִין יֵיתֵי וְיֵכוֹל. כָּל דִּצְרִיךְ יֵיתֵי וְיִפְסָח. הָשַׁתָּא הָכָא לְשָׁנָה
הַבָּאָה בְּאַרְעָא דְיִשְׂרָאֵל. הָשַׁתָּא הָכָא עַבְדֵּי לְשָׁנָה הַבָּאָה
בְּאַרְעָא דְיִשְׂרָאֵל בְּנֵי חוֹרִין:

איסטי איל פאן דילה אפריאיסייון קי קומיירון מואיסטרוס פאדריס אין **3**
טיירה די אייפטו : טודו איל קין טייני אנבֿרי בֿינגה אי

A passage from the Seder night service held on the Jewish Passover as read by Sephardic Jews of Spanish and Portuguese origin who would be Ladino speakers.

1 Hebrew in Hebrew characters.
2 Aramaic in Hebrew characters.
3 From the second word onwards (right to left) Ladino in Rabbinic characters. It reads phonetically:

> *Este (es) el pan dela afrisión (aflicción) que comieron muestros padres en tierra de Egipto. . .*

RABBINIC	PRINT	EVERYDAY	LETTER
מ	א	אָ	Aleph
נ	ב	ב	Vet
ס	ה	הָ	Hay
מ	מ	א	Mem

Throughout history learned Arabic-speaking Jews would often write to each other in Arabic, using the Hebrew script. Persian was also often written in the Hebrew script. We are now going to read English, using the Hebrew alphabet, and by the end of the chapter you will be able to read quite a bit in Hebrew and feel that using a different script and reading from right to left is not as difficult as it may at first seem. Not all the rules are covered and some have been simplified to teach the basic principles.

ב is the letter **b** and בָּ reads **ba**.

ד is the letter **d**, therefore בָּד = **bad**.

Here are some more consonants:

b = ב   **d** = ד   **g** = ג
r = ר   **n** = נ

Remember that **ָ** under a letter is **a**.

Ⓐ Now try reading these ⟵———:

בָּגְדָד   גְרָנד   גְרָב   בָּנד   בְּרָג   דְרָב

Here are the answers. Which is which?

grab, **drab**, **grand**, **band**, **brag**, **Bag(h)dad**.

Here are some more:

גְרָנדָד   בְּרָנד   רָג   בָּג   בָּר

Another two consonants: **m** = מ , **l** = ל

Another two vowels: **bed** = בֶּד   **bid** = בִּד

And a rule for using the letter **n** = נ :
If it is the last letter it is written as ן e.g. **bin** = בִּן

B Now read these:

לָנד מָדרד גרן רנג דג

Try writing these words. Remember to start from right to left.
mend, bend, mad, big, man, brag, barman, gardening

Here are some more letters with their equivalent sounds.

ִי = **y** (as in yes)
ק = **k**
ס = **s**

Now learn these vowels:
oo (u) = ◌ֻ under the letter e.g. **brood** = ברֻד
                                         rude = רֻד

o = ◌ֹ after the letter e.g. **log** = לֹג

C Can you read these words? When you decide what they sound like you will know how to spell them in English.

נֶן רֶן דָד דד קס קד בד
רֹר דֹר דָרק רֶל רֶד סָן
סל גל רֹד לד סֹר יֹר
דרֶל נל קל רֹד סד רק

D Read these names of countries or towns:

קֶנֶד סֶדָן רִיָד רֶסִי
לֹנדֹן קֹרסָק סָרדִניָ
סֶלֹן רֹמֶניָ נֹרמָנדִיָ
מָלָג מָרק דֶנמָרק

And finally, here are two new consonants:
פ = **p**
ת = **t**

59

E Read these place names.

בֶּלגְרֵי   לבֵּי   קֶנג

בֶּרמֶ   גֶרמָנִי   יָפָּן

תָסמָנִי   סקֶתלָנד   בֶּלגִי

F Can you write these in Hebrew?
Paris   Portugal   Trinidad   Glasgow

G Here are some more words for you to work out.

בֶּלד   קֶרֶב   לד   לָסת   בלָסת   גלָד

תרק   בגן   סָלָד   דסק   דסקֶתֶק

ברסתל   סָלֶת   בֶלת   בָּסקֶתבֹּל

דרְקֶל   דָלָס   לָדברֹק   סקֶל

Now here are the numbers in Hebrew. Compare them with the Arabic numbers on page 56

1 ehād

2 shenāim

3 sheloshā

4 arbaā

5 hamishā

6 shishā

7 shibaā

8 shemonā

9 tishaā

10 asarā

5 The History of English

English is spoken all over the world. The language census bar chart in Unit Two shows us that English has the second largest number of speakers in the world.

Indian women, Wular Lake

Hong Kong street scene

There are over 800 million speakers of English in the world and the numbers are continually growing. However, you will notice that only just over 410 million speak it as a *mother tongue*.

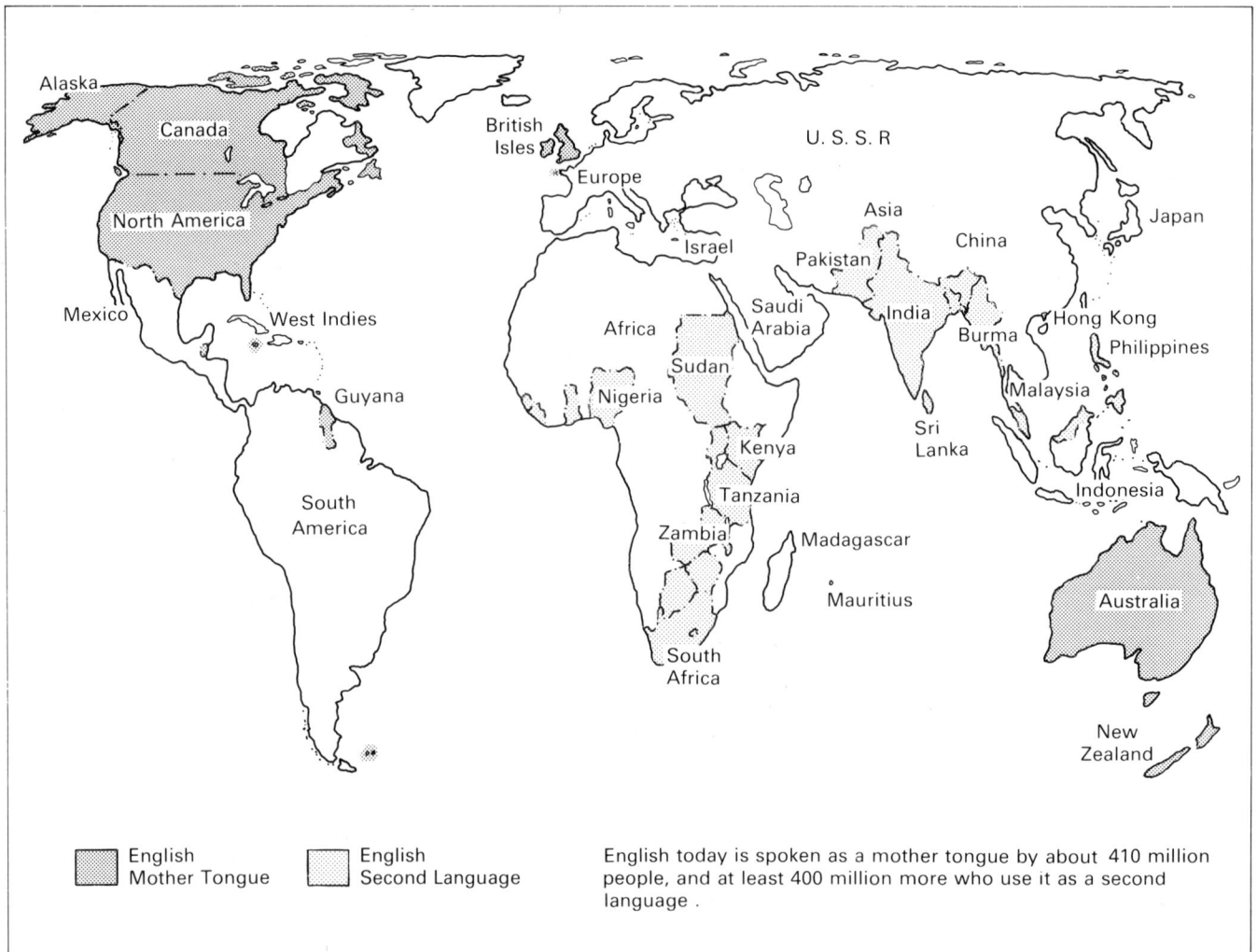

English speaking areas of the world

English today is spoken as a mother tongue by about 410 million people, and at least 400 million more who use it as a second language.

There are many varieties of English. What is formally taught to people learning English is known as *Standard English* which is by far the most usual and acceptable **written** form.

We have tried to reflect the fact that language belongs to each one of us, to the flower-seller as much as to the professor, which is of course the explanation for such popular interest: everyone uses words, even if, at first, they don't stop to think about them. But when they do, language can generate an astounding amount of heat. What is it about language that makes people so passionate, and so curious? The answer is that there is almost no aspect of our lives that is not touched by language. We live in and by language.

Extract from *The Story of English* by Robert McCrum, William Cran and Robert MacNeil p. 14, published jointly by Faber and Faber and BBC Publications © 1986.

However, *where* people live influences the language they use. Even within the UK there are a lot of regional variations and we can often tell which part of the British Isles people come from just by listening to them talking.

A Now look at the map and listen to the next six speakers. Decide where each one comes from.

Now look at the world map and listen to six more speakers. Can you work out where they all come from? Choose from the twelve countries marked on the map.

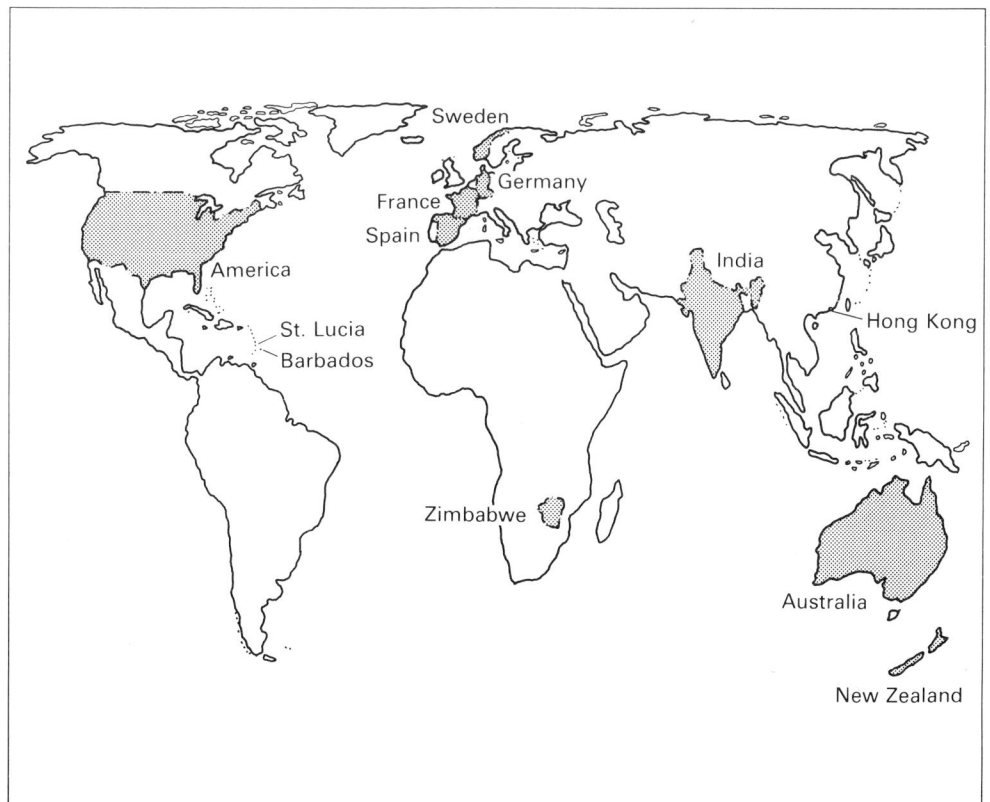

These people, in spite of speaking different varieties of English, can all understand each other quite easily.

In less than two thousand years English has grown from nothing into a language spoken by over 750 million people. This rapid rise and extensive spread are part of an extraordinary 'language success story'. So how did it happen?

Bilingual speakers

THE HISTORY OF ENGLISH

The early history of English is really a history of invasions.

The Romans

In 55 BC Julius Caesar made a rather unsuccessful invasion of the area we now call England. He found several languages spoken in this area

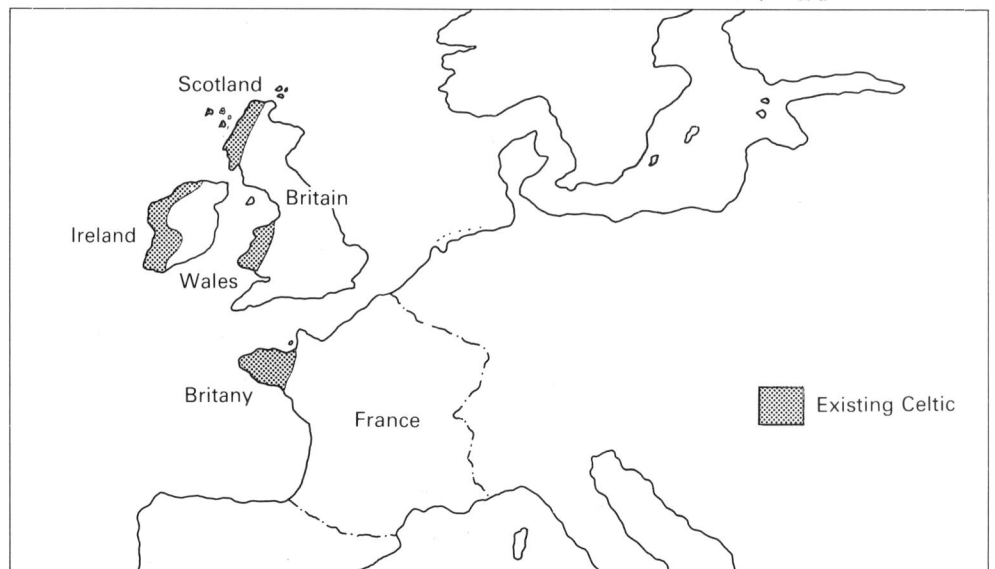

Existing Celtic speaking areas of Europe

which were all members of the Celtic language group. English did not yet exist and nor did England as we know it today. The Celtic languages were originally spoken all over Western Europe but they have largely died out. However, in Britain quite a lot of people still speak Irish, Scots Gaelic and Welsh as well as English and just a few are beginning to relearn Cornish.

The Emperor Claudius set about conquering the island in earnest in 43 AD and the Romans occupied most of the south for the next 400 years. They never succeeded in imposing their Latin language on the Celts so that in 400 AD the Celtic languages and Latin were spoken side by side in Britain. We still use a few place-names which have come from Celtic:

cumb   a deep valley
Ilfracombe, Winchcombe
tor   a high rock or peak
Torquay, Torcross

And from Latin:

castra   a camp
Manchester, Gloucester, Colchester

Apart from these there are very few words remaining from Celtic or from the early Roman invasions. Let us see why this is so.

The Angles, Saxons and Jutes

These tribes came over from Northern Europe in 449 AD. They spoke closely related Germanic languages and were very warlike and highly successful in overwhelming the Celts. We have so few Celtic words today because these invaders virtually wiped out the Celtic languages except in the extreme north and west.

'English' had arrived!

The Celts started by calling all the invaders 'Saxons' but the names *Angli*, and *Angelcynn* (Angle-kin) were also used. The language became known as *Englisc* (*Engle* from 'old English'). Finally from about 1000 AD the country was called *Englaland*.

So English came before England!

We know that English has changed enormously over the centuries and is still changing. *Anglo-Saxon* or *Old English* looks like a foreign language to modern English speakers.

Cóm on wannre niht
scríðan scadu-genga; scéotend swǽfon,
þá þæt horn-reċed healdan scoldon,
ealle bútan ánum. Þæt wæs ieldum cúþ
þæt híe ne móste, þá Meotod nolde,
sé scinn-scaða under scadu breʒdan,
ac hé wæċċende wráðum on andan
bád bolgen-mód beadwe ʒeþinges.

Gliding through the black night came the shadow walker; the warriors slept, those who should defend the gabled hall, all except one. Men knew that when the Creator did not wish it, the evil creature would not be permitted to drag them down beneath the shadows, but he (*the one*) lay vigilant, with anger against the angry one, waiting fierce-minded for the fate of the battle.

Extract from Beowulf in Anglo-Saxon, with a translation of the same passage into modern English

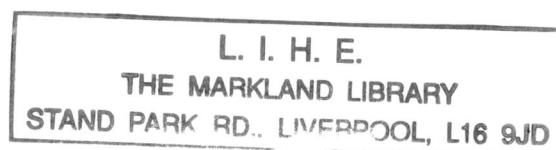

However the basic words like 'you', 'he', 'is', 'are', 'here', and 'there' are all *Anglo-Saxon* as are the rest of the hundred most commonly used words today. You could not make a natural sounding sentence today without using at least some Anglo-Saxon words. The Angles, Saxons and Jutes gave us much of our everyday vocabulary like 'wife', 'child', 'good', 'strong', 'to drink', 'to eat' and 'to sleep'. As they were farming peoples lots of our farming words came from *Anglo-Saxon*. These include: 'meadow', 'sheep', 'goat', and 'calf'.

B Your knowledge of English helps you to understand German because English is a Germanic language (via the Angles, Saxons and Jutes). Look at some modern German words and match them with the pictures.
Mutter   Haus   Wasser   Hand   Schiff   Mann

The Vikings

In 750 AD the Vikings, great seafarers who came from what is now Scandinavia, began a series of raids round the coasts of Northern Europe. They began by plundering and then actually invaded. The Vikings spoke *Old Norse* which was another Germanic-based language and when they eventually settled into the lands they had invaded, they lived alongside the 'English' speaking Saxons. Because the languages were quite similar, they found it relatively easy to understand each other but the Vikings profoundly influenced English *grammar* (the way sentences are built up). The simple sentence construction of modern English owes much to the Viking invaders.

Sometimes we still use words from both languages which have come to have slightly different meanings.

Anglo-Saxon   **Old Norse**
scyrte became 'shirt'   **skyrta** became 'skirt'

The words 'craft' and 'skill' which have the same meaning, come from Anglo-Saxon and Old Norse respectively, as do 'hide' and 'skin'.

Of course, not all Norse words begin with 'sk' but this is often a clue to us that a word might have come from Old Norse. It has also given us many other ordinary everyday words, such as: 'husband', 'sister', 'window', 'egg', 'bloom', 'leg', and 'get' as well as some place names ending in:

-by (farm)
Grimsby
Derby and *Rugby*

thorp (village)
Cleethorpes
Maplethorpe and *Althorpe*

The Normans

Soon after the decline of Viking power in Northern Europe, the English language had to survive yet another invasion. In 1066 AD William of Normandy landed at Pevensey and defeated King Harold at Hastings. Harold was the last English speaking king for nearly 300 years and the chart of the early invasions was complete.

Date	Invaders	Language	Example of words
55 BC and 43 AD	Romans	Latin	very few (mainly place names)
449 AD	Angles Saxons and Jutes	Anglo-Saxon	fish, cow, earth
800 AD	Vikings	Old Norse	whisk, weak, root
1066 AD	Normans	Norman French	reign, battle, accuse

C Below is a map of Northern Europe showing the movements of the early invaders. Make a list of the modern names of the countries marked. What are the names and dates of invaders A, B and C?

The language spoken by the Normans was quite different from Anglo-Saxon and Old Norse. It was one of the varieties of French, a

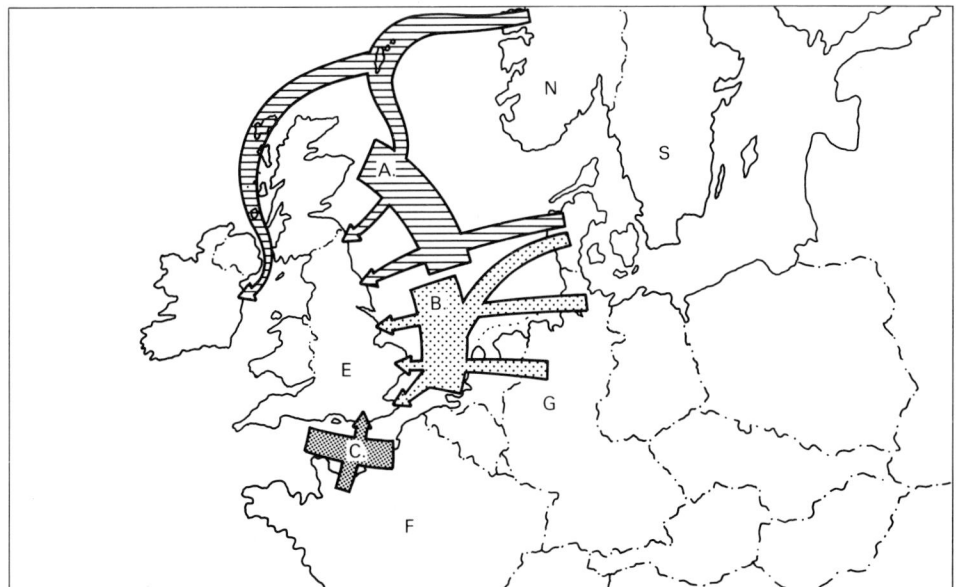

Romance language, a descendant of Latin and not a Germanic language at all. You can find out a lot more about *Romance* languages in the next unit.

Ordinary people went on speaking English which was already very well-established. The invaders, of course, spoke *Norman French* but they soon began to settle down, think of England as their home, marry English wives, deal with English peasants and learn some English. But Latin and French were the languages of government, of the law, of literature, and of fashion. They therefore introduced many words to do with these subjects.

Government and administration
crown   treasurer   tax   messenger   parliament

Law
judge   petition   jury   ransom   assault

Fashion
robe   cape   embroidery   satin   pleat

The nobles all continued to use French and as they commanded the army many military words we use today come from French.

Nobility
noble   baron   viscount   princess   sir

Army and Navy
siege   defence   soldier   moat   enemy

There was a clear class distinction between Anglo-Saxon and French under Norman rule. It was definitely fashionable to speak French!

LATIN: INVASION OR CULTURAL REVOLUTION?

We have looked at four invasions of Britain: the Romans, the Angles, Saxons and Jutes, the Vikings and the Normans. Three of these invasions made major contributions to the language we speak today but the Roman invasions of Julius Caesar and Claudius seem to have left little linguistic trace. Does this mean we do not use any words derived from Latin?

D Look up these words in an *etymological dictionary* and see how many of them come from Latin:

cucumber   millet   carrot   oyster   herb

Now what about these:
angel   bishop   convent   demon   crucifix

Invading armies are not the only people to spread words. Trade is another powerful word carrier.

Now look again at the second list above. All these are 'religion-related' words. The majority of Latin words that have come into English have come in through the influence of the Church. Christianity was introduced into Britain in 597 and Latin borrowings continued to make their way into the language over the next five hundred years. *Everyday words* from Latin also came in because of the influence of the Church. Our first group of words above has nothing to do with religion but a lot to do with food!

English continued to borrow from Latin throughout the years of Norman rule. It is difficult for us to detect, however, whether a 'borrowed' word reached us directly from Latin or through Norman French, which was Latin based.

E Sammy's Uncle Charles is always trying to teach him to speak more formally (using words from Latin or French) while Sammy is quite happy with his less formal words of Germanic origin. Read this conversation and write it out in your own books with the blanks filled in. The first one is an example.

Sammy	Uncle Charles
Where did you *get* that hat?	I *acquired* it from an acquaintance.
It must have been *dear*.	Yes, I believe it was rather . . . .
Do you know my friend saw a . . . . the other day.	My dear boy, I don't believe in *apparitions*.
But he said it . . . . him home.	Really! How can one be *pursued* by an apparition?
But it did! He was really	Yes, I expect one would be rather *terrified*.
Eventually he . . . . a tree.	Did he think apparitions cannot *ascend* trees then?
But he had to *come down* in the end.	I suppose he would have to . . . . He couldn't stay there all night.
Then he had an idea. He pretended that he had . . . . of fright.	Oh, that's very drole. So, did the apparition think he had *expired*?
Yes, it *went away* and he had no more trouble after that.	So the apparition . . . . What a story!

Now look up all the italicised words in an etymological dictionary. You will find that the more informal words are of Old English or Germanic origin, whereas the more formal words come from Latin or French.

F Below is a list of some more Latin or French derived words that Sammy's Uncle wants him to use. Can you complete, in your exercise books, the list of *Anglo-Saxon verbs* that have the same meanings?

Latin or French	Anglo-Saxon
to aid	to help
to commence	
to cease	
to prepare	
to increase	
to extend	
to reject	
to enter	
to exit	

Do you notice anything interesting about the last five *Anglo-Saxon verbs*?
Now write eight sentences using the eight words above from Latin or French.
Try to make sure your sentences show that you understand the meaning of each word.

G One day Uncle Charles wrote a fairy-story for Sammy's younger brother and sister. As usual, it was full of words from French and Latin. Sammy wanted to make some changes. He thought the style was much too formal. Rewrite the story changing the italicised words to more suitable words for this kind of tale.

> Once upon a time Esmeralda was *presented* with a *beautiful object* by her *beau*. The *audacious* and *affectionate* young man had *endured* much in *extracting* it from a haunted *mansion*. He had *laboured* to *conquer* everything although he was almost forced to *surrender* when *pursued* by a *ferocious* beast. But he *concealed* himself behind a tree and the beast *departed*. His wounds were not *profound*. Esmeralda *purged* them and after this they *cohabited* happily ever after.

H Are words from French or Latin always formal? Look again at the list from exercise D.

cucumber   millet   carrot   oyster   herb

Now look at the list below. Which set of words comes from Latin/French?

cell	prison
fool	idiot
furious	irate
calm	tranquil
enormous	colossal

When you have decided, check them in an etymological dictionary. What did you find? What conclusions can you draw?

WRITTEN ENGLISH

From 1066 to about 1500, the English in use is called Middle English. During this period the spoken languages developed differently in different parts of the country. There were various words for the same objects, and pronunciation varied considerably. The five main dialects of Middle English are the South Western, the South Eastern, the East Midland, the West Midland and the Northern dialects. It was the East Midland dialect which gradually spread in use and was the basis of present-day Standard English.

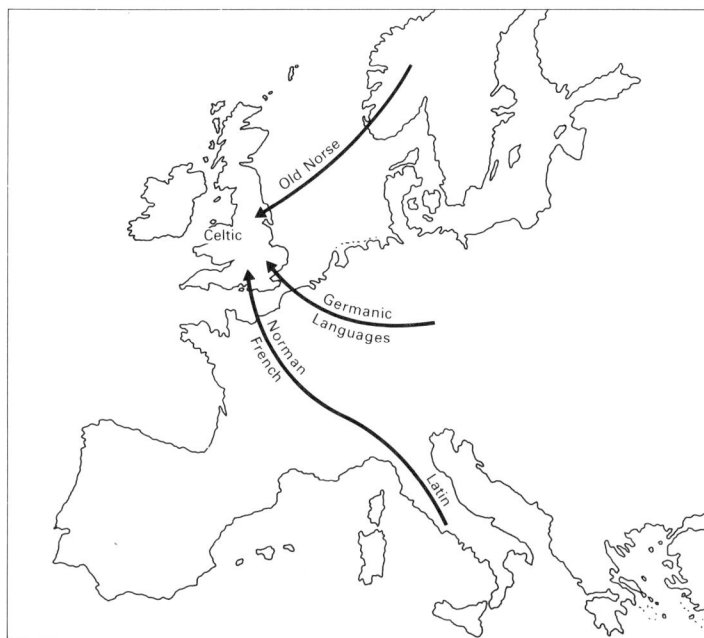

Middle English dialects 1500

From Spoken to Written

English is well known for the difficulty of its spelling. The same sound may be written in many different ways, (e.g. the *aw* sound in 'claw', 'door', 'more', 'four' is spelt in a different way in each word.) In addition, we also have whole words in English with identical pronunciation but which are not spelt the same way.

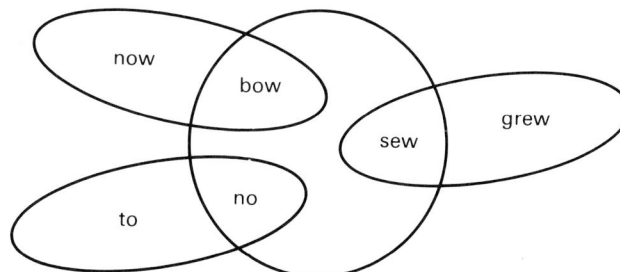

I Find an English word which sounds the same as each of the words given but which is spelt differently. The first one has been done for you. Write the answers in your exercise books.

1 write – right
2 bough
3 doe
4 hear
5 there

6 so
7 threw
8 which
9 site
10 pair

Use the clues below to help you find ten English words, all of which contain an 'oo' sound (as in 'too'). Each 'oo' sound is spelt differently. Write the answers in your books.

1 Me and . . . . (= we).
2 One . . . . three.
3 To keep alive we eat . . . .
4 You go across the river and then . . . . the wood.
5 I am going . . . . London.
6 W. . . . . . . are you?
7 The French flag is red, white and . . . .
8 Her new . . . . have very high heels.
9 The beanstalk just g. . . . . . . and g. . . . .
10 The government has changed after a military c. . . . .

Let us look at some early spelling.

J Borrow a copy of *Beowulf* or Chaucer's *Canterbury Tales* from the library. Both these examples of early English literature were written before the printing press was in general use. Make a list of words you recognise and add the modern spellings next to each one.

> Bifel that, in that seson on a day,
> In Southwerk at the Tabard as I lay
> Redy to wenden on my pilgrimage
> To Caunterbury with ful devout corage,
> At night was come in-to that hostelrye
> Wel nyne and twenty in a companye,
> Of sondry folk, by aventure y-falle
> In felawshipe, and pilgrims were they alle,
> That toward Caunterbury wolden ryde;
> The chambres and the stables weren wyde,
> And wel we weren esed atte beste.
> And shortly, whan the sonne was to reste,
> So hadde I spoken with hem everichon,
> That I was of hir felawshipe anon,
> And made forward erly for to ryse,
> To take our wey, there as I yow devyse.

Geoffrey Chaucer. *The Canterbury Tales: The General Prologue*, lines 19–34

With the advent of printing, spelling became more regular. The first book to be printed in England was produced by William Caxton. Until that time manuscripts had to be copied out by hand; consequently very little written material was available. The invention of the printing press changed all this. It meant that books became accessible to some people who until then had little or no contact with the written language.

Interior of a printing-press workshop, by Abraham von Werdt of Nuremberg, 1678

William Caxton decided for himself what spelling he preferred and in many cases his choice became the official spelling. Having spent much of his life in Holland he was very influenced by Dutch spellings and as a result, for example, we spell the word 'aghast' with a **g** before the *h* because a number of Dutch words are spelt with a **gh**. Latin was a very strong influence on the early printers who all received an education in the classical languages; consequently they frequently chose spellings based on the Latin roots of English words. Some of these also have silent letters. Examples of this are 'scene' from Latin *scena*, and 'receipt' from *recipere* where the **c** and **p** respectively have been kept even though they are not sounded in the English word.

K Read the clues below and find the words. They all derive from Latin or Greek and include a 'silent' letter. Write out the words and underline the unsounded letter in each word:

1 R. . . . . . . = measure of beats in music or poetry.
2 R. . . . . . . = large African or South Asiatic animal with one or two horns and very thick skin.
3 C. . . . . . = a group of singers.
4 C. . . . . . = a combination of 3 or more musical notes played together according to the rules of harmony.
5 P. . . . . . = serious illness which is an inflammation of the lungs.
6 P. . . . . . = functions by means of wind or air (e.g. a p. . . . . . drill).
7 P. . . . . . = a person who repairs pipes, drains etc.
8 R. . . . . . = the period during which a sovereign rules.

L Make a list of as many words as you can which use the Greek **ph** for an **f** sound; e.g. tele**ph**one.

In languages, such as French and Spanish, committees of scholars were set up to decide on one final form of spelling and to make rules about how the language should be correctly used. English did not have such committees and so it was left to printers and writers of dictionaries to attempt to standardise the spelling of English. People such as Dr Samuel Johnson have had an important influence on English spelling. (Dr Johnson produced one of the first dictionaries of the English language in the eighteenth century. It took him eight years to compile). However, English remains a language with very irregular spelling.

A meeting of the Académie française, a group of French scholars who first met in 1634 to establish rules of French spelling and grammar

M 1 With the help of reference books, find out all you can about the invention of printing.
2 Look up the words 'lexicography' and 'lexicographer' in the dictionary. Try to find out from which Greek stem-word they have come.

We can see that English has both Germanic (Anglo Saxon) and Romance (Old French and Latin) roots and we can see that these varied influences make it a richer language. Yet it was not only in its early period that English borrowed words. Like many other languages English has continued to borrow.

N So many English words have an interesting story behind them. The boxes on the following page contain some of those stories. Can you match these explanations with the words to which they belong?
bungalow, sputnik, ghetto, potato, dock, castle, tea, blitz.

From one of the *Chinese* dialects, this word came into *Malay* then into *Dutch*. It was used in England in the seventeenth century when the drink was first imported into Europe.

Dutch. This word, like a number of other words to do with the sea, sailing and boating, came into English in the fifteenth to sixteenth centuries from Britain's seafaring neighbours, the Dutch.

French. When William the Conqueror invaded England in 1066, the Normans brought with them many new military ideas such as defences which included a stone rampart and stone towers.

German. This word was used during World War II in the 1940s. The German word means 'lightning flash' and was used particularly to describe the air attack on London in 1940–41.

Italian. This was originally the name of the part of Venice where the Jewish community was forced to live, away from the rest of the town. It has since been extended to mean the quarters of a particular minority group in a city, usually the poorest communities.

Hindi/Bengali. People from the British East India Company came to India in the seventeenth century to trade there. The one-storied houses they stayed in were called 'bangla' or 'bangalo' in Hindi or Bengali.

Spanish. Spanish explorers in South America were the first Europeans to eat this vegetable which they found there. The Spanish word came into English in the sixteenth century when they were brought to Europe by Spanish and English explorers, such as Walter Raleigh.

Russian. This word means 'traveller' and was used to name a series of unmanned earth satellites launched into space by Russia in the 1950s.

English has borrowed words from all over the world. Look at the world map below and match up the words which are printed in their country of origin, with the language from which they have come.

English word	Language of origin	Meaning of original
tycoon	Japanese	great lord
	Russian	little water
	Sanskrit	lord of the world
	Icelandic	small cask
	Arabic	sugar solution
	Swahili	expedition
	Eskimo	seal-skin canoe
	Haitian	corn
	Persian	loose cover over shoulders
	Nahuatl (Aztecs)	plant with edible red fruit
	Finnish	steam bath
	N. American Indian	woman or wife

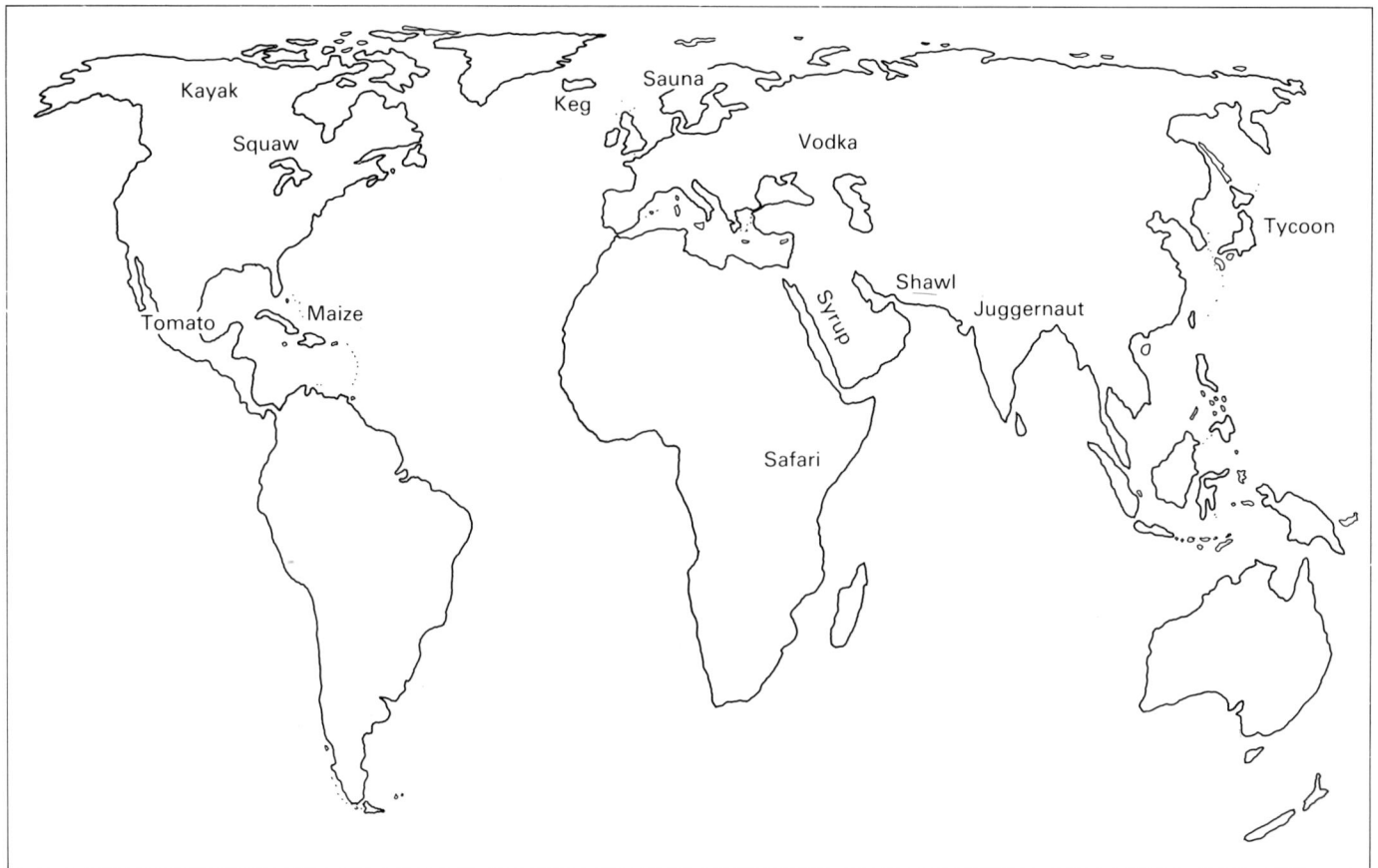

English has spread remarkably over the past 500 years. No other language has become so widespread. In fact, just as Anglo-Saxon practically wiped out the Celtic languages spoken in England, so English has often taken over from the original languages of the countries colonised by Britain to become the official or principal language used. It is the principal language of thirty-four countries and spoken as a second language in dozens of other countries.

P 1 Find out all the countries where English is the official language.

2 When you have found this out, see if you can discover the name of some of the original or *indigenous* languages of these countries.

3 If you have speakers from other English speaking countries in your class, find out if they can tell you any differences between the way English is used in their countries and the way you speak. Think whether these are differences in *accent*, *vocabulary* or *intonation*.

4 If you can speak a dialect or a variety of English, write down a few sentences of your speech trying to spell the words exactly as they sound to you phonetically. Now write your sentences again, but this time with standard English spellings.

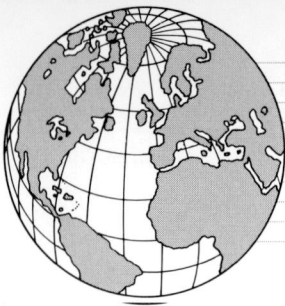

6 Romance Languages

The Spanish, Portuguese, French, Italian, Rumanian, Provençal, Catalan and Romansch languages have many characteristics in common. They make up one group within the much larger family of Indo-European languages and are all known by the name *Romance languages.*

Rumanian	French	Spanish	Portuguese	Italian	Provençal	English
curs	cours	curso	curso	corso	cors	course
negru	noir	negro	negro	nero	negro	black
natură	nature	naturaleza	natureza	natura	natura	nature
medic	médicin	médico	médico	medico	medecin	doctor
capră	chèvre	cabra	cabra	capra	cabro	goat
cînta	chanter	cantar	cantar	cantare	cantaire	to sing
autocamion	camion	camión	camião	camion	camioun	lorry
barbă	barbe	barba	barba	barba	barbetto	beard
amabil	aimable	amable	amável	amabile	amador	likeable

A Look at the map below and consider if a clue to their shared characteristics is contained within it.

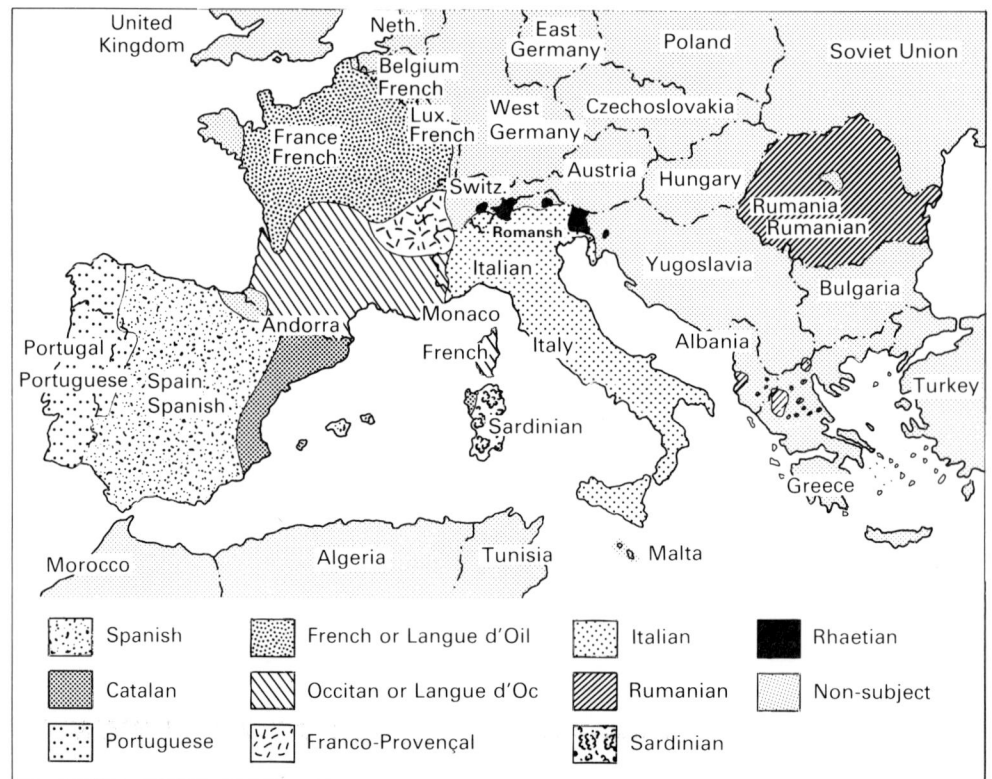

Romance languages of Europe

Why should the name Romance have been chosen? Surely we cannot claim that all speakers of these languages are romantic by nature? The answer lies in the name itself – ROMAN (CE). This dissecting of words to find new meaning and common understanding is the basis of what we shall be looking at in this unit.

Roman is the word used to describe anything to do with the people and history of the Roman Empire, which was based obviously enough in the ancient city of Rome. The language of this vast Empire was *Latin*.

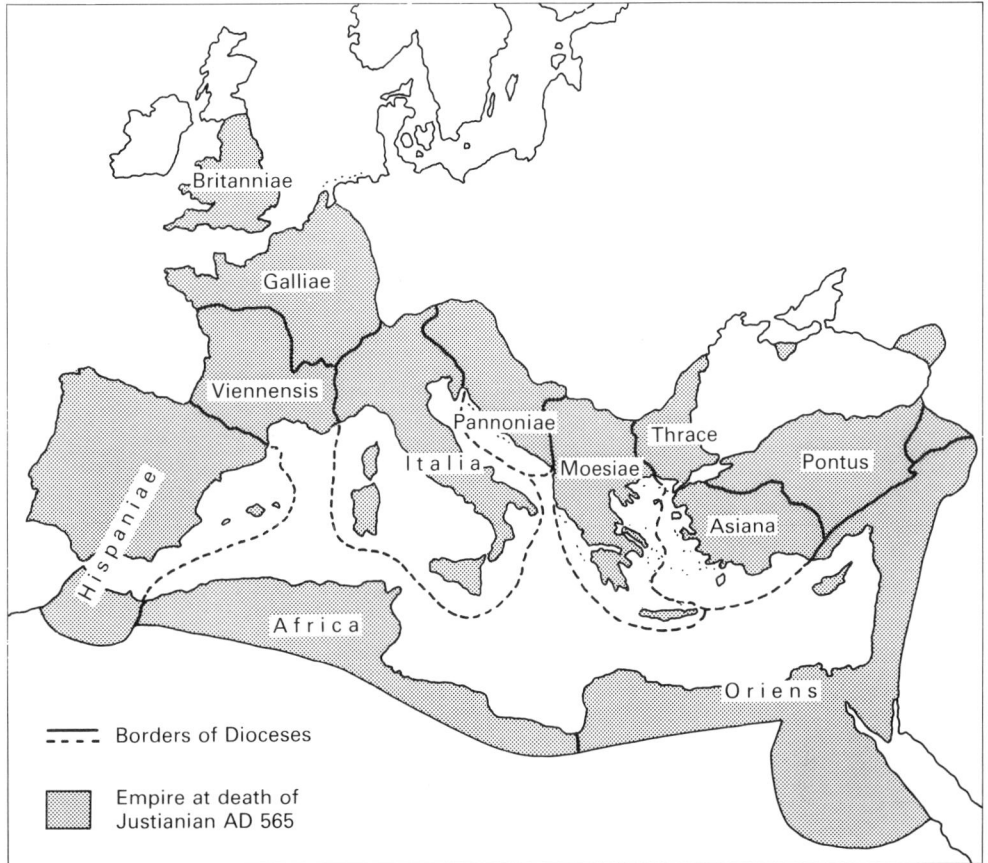

Britanniae

Galliae

Viennensis

Pannoniae

Hispaniae

Italia

Moesiae

Thrace

Pontus

Asiana

Africa

Oriens

------- Borders of Dioceses

Empire at death of
Justianian AD 565

Extent of the Roman Empire at the death of Emperor Justinian AD 565

By now you will have realised that the areas in which the Romance languages are spoken were, at one time, all part of this powerful empire. Empires are built when a nation acquires foreign territory either by force of arms or agreement, and in this case, the Roman armies conquered a large part of the 'known' world of that time. Can you imagine how difficult it must have been to govern such a vast area of land without the benefits of the telephone and computer and when the fastest means of transport was the horse?

"What do we do now, Caesar?"

LONDINIUM
← MCLXVI

What immense organisation it must have required to control so much land, so many people and such an army. Given these factors, what must have been the most important means for the Roman Empire of ensuring the control of its territories? The answer has to be *language*. By imposing your language on another country and conducting all communication in it, you are using a most potent form of control. In the case of the Roman Empire, language played a most important role. As the legions marched forward, another army of administrators, engineers and academics was close behind, establishing new legal and governing systems, building a network of efficient communications and establishing Latin as the most significant and vital language.

You may now ask what happened to the languages of the original inhabitants of these newly conquered areas of the Roman Empire? Gradually as the Roman armies established their position and created systems to maintain it, Latin, the language of the all-powerful conqueror, blended with the native tongues and each area developed a new language with a Latin core.

At this stage it is important to note that the language used by the common Roman soldier and therefore the one acquired by the new citizens of their Empire, was not the same Latin as used by poets and scholars or in official state documents. Use of classical Latin by academics and within the Church ensured its survival in its written form but by the collapse of the Roman Empire in 476 AD Vulgar Latin was the everyday speech of the conquered areas. This then modified into the Romance languages of today.

By referring back to the map of the Roman Empire you will see that in 55–54 BC parts of Britain were conquered by the Romans, but we did not include English in the original list of Romance languages. It was only much later that Latin had a significant effect on English but was eventually only one of many sources of new vocabulary, whilst in the areas of the Romance languages, Latin was not only the predominant influence, but the core on which they were built.

The earliest written examples of these Romance languages were discovered in the following centuries:

French	ninth century
Spanish, Italian	tenth century
Provençal, Portuguese	twelfth century
Catalan	twelfth century
Rumanian	sixteenth century

By referring back now to the map of Romance languages, you will see that Rumania is geographically isolated from the core area of the other Romance languages. The influence of Latin, however, is still significant, especially given the fact that the Romans were only there for 165 years to consolidate their borders. Moreover, the area suffered continual invasions from the Germanic, Slavonic and Magyar peoples who contributed considerable vocabulary to Rumanian, just as the Arabs had done in Spain during their occupation between the years of 711–1492.

CLXXV

Ço sent Rollant, de sun tens n'i ad plus;
Devers Espaigne est en un pui agut,
A l'une main si ad sun piz batud:
'Deus, meie culpe vers les tues vertuz!
2370 De mes pecchez, des granz e des menuz,
Que jo ai fait des l'ure que nez fui
Tresqu'a' cest jur que ci sui consoüt!'
Sun destre guant en ad vers Deu tendut.
Angles del ciel i descendent a lui. Aoi.

CLXXVI

2375 Li quens Rollant se jut desuz un pin,
Envers Espaigne en ad turnét sun vis;
De plusurs choses a remembrer li prist:
De tantes teres cum li bers conquist,
De dulce France, des humes de sun lign,
2380 De Carlemagne, sun seignor ki·l nurrit;
Ne poet müer n'en plurt e ne suspirt;
Mais lui meïsme ne volt mettre en ubli,

La Chanson de Roland, twelfth
century, lines 2366–2382

The extent of the influence of Latin is now no longer confined to Europe. By the sixteenth century the Spanish, Portuguese and French had conquered South and Central America and the Caribbean and there are now nearly 700 million people who speak, as their mother tongue, a language genetically related to Latin. The non-European Romance language speakers outnumber their European counterparts two to one. Yet despite the geographical spread of Romance languages, the Latin influence remains because there is, in terms of vocabulary, a forty per cent core, common to all. This percentage increases to sixty-five per cent between French and Spanish, and ninety between Spanish and Portuguese.

Latin	Rumanian	Spanish	Portuguese	Italian	French	English
multus	mult	mucho	muito	molto	beaucoup	much
fames	foame	hambre	fome	fame	faim	hunger
cogitara	gîndi	pensar	pensar	pensare	penser	to think
sed	ci	pero	mais	ma	mais	but
hic	aici	aquí	aquí	qui	ici	here

However, although this high degree of shared vocabulary can be recognised in the written form, it is not necessarily so when spoken.

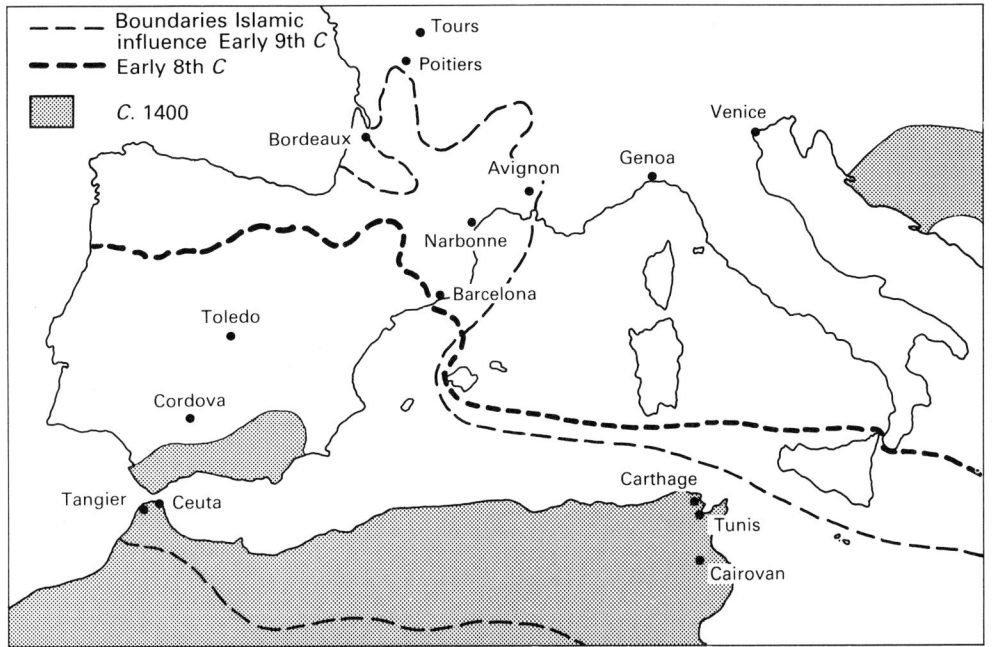

Boundaries Islamic influence Early 9th *C*
Early 8th *C*
C. 1400

Tours
Poitiers
Venice
Bordeaux
Avignon
Genoa
Narbonne
Barcelona
Toledo
Cordova
Tangier • Ceuta
Carthage
Tunis
Cairovan

Extent of Arabic conquests in Spain 1400

U.S.A.

Haiti
Puerto Rico
Guadeloupe
Caribbean Sea
Dominica
Martinique
St. Lucia
Aruba • Curacao

Mexico
Cuba
Dominican Republic
Belize
Honduras
Guatemala
Nicaragua
El Salvador
Costa Rica
Panama
Guyana
Surinam
Venezuela
French Guyana
Colombia
Ecuador
Peru
Brazil
Bolivia
Paraguay
Chile
Uruguay
Argentina
Falklands

Spanish
Portuguese
French/Portuguese
French
Dutch
English

European linguistic influence in Central and South America

The name *cognate* is given to words sharing a common root. There are many *cognates* across any two of the Romance languages. We are now going to work in six of these languages: Latin, French, Spanish, Italian, Portuguese and Rumanian.

Español
Français
Italiano
Portugues
Limba Română
Latinus

ROMANCE LANGUAGES WORKSHOP
For Students who have a background in either French, Spanish, Portuguese or Italian. Students use their knowledge of one language in order to study the others by the comparative method
Q3042 Romance Languages Workshop
Mon 7.00-9.00 P. O'Leary

B Which languages can you identify without any help?

1 Il pagamento avviere su presentazione di nota alla fine di settimana.
2 On paie sur présentation de la note à la fin de la semaine.
3 Em Lisboa come-se bem. Toda a gente o sabe.
4 En Valencia se vive bien. Todo el mundo lo sabe.
5 Agnus lupum non amat.
6 Eu sint elev in clase a cincea.
Your teacher will tell you which is which.

Here is a vocabulary list in French:

tout – all	**aimer** – to love/to like
bien – well	**non** – no
savoir – to know	**classe** – class
vivre – to live	**loup** – wolf
élève – pupil	**tout le monde** – everyone
cinq – five	**gens** – people
agneau – lamb	**comestible** – edible

By reading this list you should now be able to work out what sentences 3, 4, 5 and 6 mean.
If your teacher speaks French and/or Spanish, then 1 and 2 can be done as well. Did you notice that the 'v' in **savoir** in French is a 'b' in Spanish and Portuguese?

C Here is a vocabulary list in Spanish:

voy – I am going	**trabajar** – to work
billetes – tickets	**horas** – hours
comprar – to buy	**once** – eleven
vino – wine	**comenzar** – to begin
la cuenta – the bill	**el cliente** – the client

Now try and work these out with the help of your Spanish and French vocabulary:

Rumanian: Voi cumpăra biletele.
French: Michel commence à travailler à onze heures.
Portuguese: Maria compra o vinho.
Italian: Il cliente non paga il conto.
Latin: Ad poetam scribo.

Did you notice that Latin has the verb at the end of the sentence? (To the poet I write.)

D   Now here is a list of vocabulary in Rumanian:

cravată – tie	**voi** – I am going
decembrie – December	**intra** – to go in
doctor – doctor	**maior** – major
grandios – grandiose	**floare** – flower
jurnal – newspaper	**viu** – living
lăuda – to praise	**cîmp** – field
cumpăra – to buy	**port** – harbour
agricultor – farmer	**nord** – north
mamă – mother	**mînă** – hand

Now the following sentences should be easy to understand.

Spanish: En diciembre voy a comprar flores para mi mamá.
Latin: Poeta agricolam laudat.
French: Le docteur entre, le journal à la main.
Portuguese: A grande maioria das familias vive do campo.
Italian: La maggior parte del porto è nel nord.

les nits són fredes

TREBALLEU PER AL FRONT

P.S.U.

How good is your Catalan?

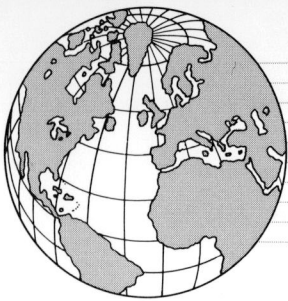

7 Russian

In this unit, we are going to look at some of the differences between the Russian language and most of the other languages you have met so far. By the time you reach the end of the unit, you will be able to read and write some Russian and recognise some words when spoken in Russian, as well as say them yourself.

But, before you begin, think about what Russian means to you. Who are the Russians? Where is Russia? What is life like in Russia? We all have our own ideas about countries or people we have never met. These ideas are often based on prejudice or on impressions gained from the television.

(A) 1 What do you think of when you hear the words Russia or Russians? Write down some of the things that immediately spring to your mind, or draw some of your ideas.
2 Now compare your list with a partner's one. Did you have similar ideas? Do you think these give a true picture of Russia and the people who live there?

It is possible that you have never met anyone who comes from Russia, so you can only build up your picture of the country and its people from the information you read or see in the media, or get second-hand from someone else. As only two million people visit the Soviet Union each year, even this information may not be acccurate. We hope that the work you do in this unit will help you build a truer image of Russia and the Russians. Who knows, some of you may even decide to visit Russia or go on to study the language!

THE USSR

Before looking at the Russian language, let us think briefly about where Russia is, and consider again your answer to exercise A. In fact, 'Russia' is only one of fifteen republics that together form the USSR (the Union of Soviet Socialist Republics). Look at this map and you will see that the Russian republic is the largest one.

You will also notice from the small inset map of the world how enormous the USSR is. Together, the fifteen soviet republics cover one sixth of the land on earth – 8,602,700 square miles! If you were to measure the distance from the far west to the far east of the USSR, it would come to nearly 12,000 miles. If you travelled along this line, the countryside would change from the extensive grassy plains of the steppes to mountains and forests. From the north to the south, you

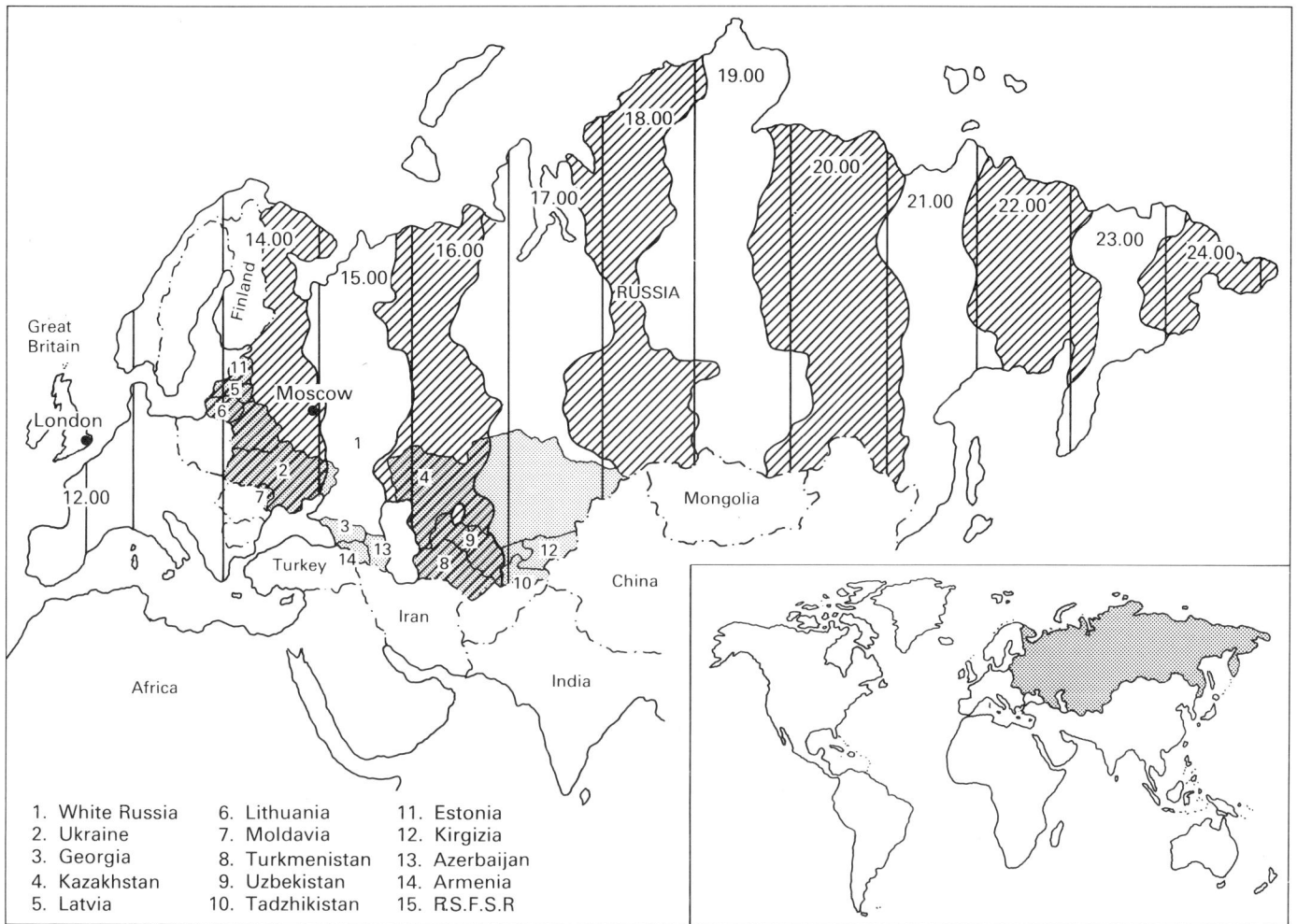

1. White Russia	6. Lithuania	11. Estonia
2. Ukraine	7. Moldavia	12. Kirgizia
3. Georgia	8. Turkmenistan	13. Azerbaijan
4. Kazakhstan	9. Uzbekistan	14. Armenia
5. Latvia	10. Tadzhikistan	15. R.S.F.S.R

would pass from arctic to desert regions, and you would find 225,000 miles of river in the Soviet Union.

So, the USSR is a vast country, made up of many states, which have different climates and do not even share the same time. For example, when it is midday on Monday in London, it is 2 p.m. in Moscow, but 7 p.m. in central parts of the Soviet Union, and 1 a.m. on Tuesday in eastern regions of the country!

You might expect people who live in such different environments to have different ways of life, produce different goods, eat different food, and even have different appearances. Look at the photographs on page 88 of some Soviet citizens. Do they match the ideas you had about Russians in exercise A?. In fact, there are 115 different nationalities in the Soviet Union, and these are just some of them.

Another idea you might have mentioned in your answer to exercise A concerns political stereotypes: ideas of spies, stories of Russians and Americans trying to rival each other, people wanting to escape from their life in the Soviet Union. But how do 'glasnost' and 'perestroika' fit into this view? Will this new openness now allow us to see past the stereotypes and increase our knowledge of Russia beyond the following list of well known facts?

Men in a Tashkent teahouse,
Uzbekistan

Men standing at the entrance to
Shahi-Zinda mausoleum,
Samarkland, Uzbekistan

Mrs Gorbachev visiting a London
school, December 1987

The vegetable market, Yalta, Crimea

Tadjik farming woman

- The first man to go into space and return safely was a Russian.
- The Russians are world champions in many sports, such as gymnastics and ice-skating.
- Some of the greatest writers in history are from the USSR. Can you think of the name of one of Tolstoy's works?
- Moscow has one of the finest ballets in the world, the Bolshoi.
- Russia and Britain were allies in the Second World War.

B Can you guess which parts of the USSR the people on page 88 come from? Give a reason for your answers. What sort of life-style do you think they have? What do they do for a living? What sort of homes do they have?

THE DEVELOPMENT OF THE RUSSIAN LANGUAGE

You should now be able to picture the part of the world where Russian is spoken, but how did the language develop? Indeed, do the different peoples of the USSR even speak the same language? The earliest piece of written Russian that has been found dates back to the eleventh century. At that time, there were three different forms of Russian in use:
– spoken Russian, known as 'Old Russian',
– the written form of 'Old Russian',
– a second written form, used only for religious purposes.

Today, most people in the USSR speak both Russian and the language of their own republic. The table below shows some of these languages. How does it relate to your knowledge of language families?

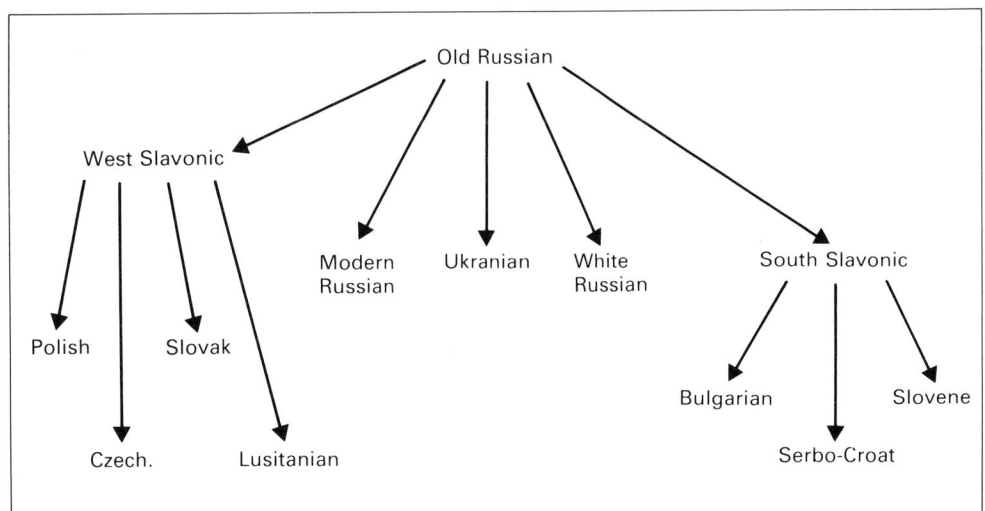

Languages based on Old Russian

One of the difficulties we have in learning Russian is that it does not use the Roman alphabet which English, French, Spanish and most European languages use. Instead, it uses the Cyrillic script, which we shall meet shortly.

Answer the following questions and see how much you can remember so far about the Russian language, people and republics.

1 What do the initials USSR stand for?
2 Are there five, ten or fifteen states in the Soviet Union?
3 Do these states all speak Russian only, or do they speak different languages?
4 How many forms of Russian were there in the eleventh century?
5 Give the name of one language, apart from modern Russian, that Old Russian developed into.
6 Does Russian use the Cyrillic alphabet or the Roman alphabet?
7 What was the title of the Russian king?
8 Why is Yuri Gagarin famous?
9 Was Tolstoy a great Russian politician, writer or ballet dancer?
10 What is Petrograd the old name for?
11 Is time in eastern regions of the USSR ahead of or behind time in the west?
12 In which city is the Kremlin to be found?
13 What is the name of the Russian premier?

THE RUSSIAN LANGUAGE РУСКИЙ ЯЗЫК

You learnt in the introduction that Russian uses the Cyrillic alphabet. This consists of thirty-two letters. Some of them have the same sound as they have in English, but some are pronounced differently to what you might expect. There are also some sounds for which we do not have a letter in English.

Like English, Russian has different forms for printing and hand-writing, but we are going to concentrate only on the printed letters. Set out below are all the letters of the Russian alphabet. The first column shows you how to print the capital and small letters. The second column tells you how to pronounce each letter.

Letter		Pronunciation
А	а	ah
Б	б	b
В	в	v
Г	г	g
Д	д	d
Е	е	ye
Ё	ё	yo
Ж	ж	zh (as in plea*s*ure)
З	з	z
И	и	ee
Й	й	y (as in bo*y*)
К	к	k
Л	л	l
М	м	m
Н	н	n
О	о	o
П	п	p
Р	р	r
С	с	s
Т	т	t
У	у	oo
Ф	ф	f
Х	х	ch (as in lo*ch*)
Ц	ц	ts (as in bi*ts*)
Ч	ч	ch
Ш	ш	sh
Щ	щ	shch
Ъ	ъ	[silent - hard sign]
Ы	ы	i (as in oe*i*l)
Ь	ь	[silent - soft sign]
Э	э	e (as in b*e*t)
Ю	ю	you
Я	я	ya

D Listen to the tape and compare the words you hear with the way they are written. There are pauses on the tape for you to repeat each word.

1 **футбол**
2 **стадион**
3 **хоккей**
4 **Ленинград**
5 **Москва**

Did you spot some of the new letters and some of those that have different sounds from their English equivalents?

Some facts about Russian

Russian has thirty-two letters.
There are five vowels as in English, but each one has both a hard and a soft form.

	hard	soft
e.g. a	**а**	**о**
e	**э**	**e**

There are two letters that have no sound of their own. They are just used to tell us how to pronounce the letter that precedes them. They are known as 'hard' and 'soft' signs, and are written as **ъ** and **ь**.

Some words are spelt the same in Russian and English. By changing the letters from one script to the other, you can work out their meanings.

E Listen to the tape and decide which answer you think matches what you hear.

e.g. **a** 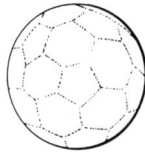 **b**  **c**

1 a  **b**  **c**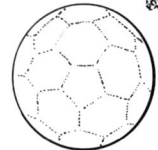

2 a 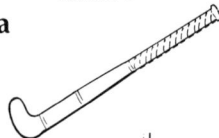 **b** 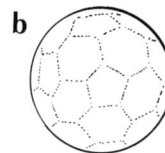 **c**

3 a 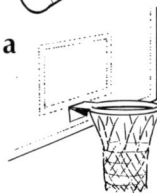 **b** 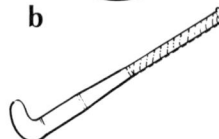 **c**

4 a ЛЕНИНГРАД   **b** МОСКВА   **c** ЛОНДОН

5 a МИНСК   **b** ЯЛТА   **c** МОСКВА

F Use the alphabet listed earlier in this unit to help you find the answers to these questions.

1 Find three letters that are spelt and sound the same in both Russian and English.

2 Now find three letters that look like English letters but have different sounds in Russian.

3 How many letters can you find for sounds that we do not have in the Roman alphabet?

G да? нет? Listen to the tape. If the word you hear matches the printed word, write **да** (yes). If not, write **нет** (no).

1 спорт
2 телеграмма
3 кофе
4 лампа
5 турист

H Listen to the tape again and see if you can write down the words you hear. Write your answers in your exercise book. All the spellings you need are in the following box.

Москва	Лондон	Парйж	Нью Иорк	Берлйн

I Practise writing some Russian by matching the Russian and English words for sports listed in the boxes below.

football
tennis
hockey
cricket
sport

спорт
крйкет
теннис
хоккей
футбол

J Listen to the tape and try to write down the place names (1–5) you hear, using Russian letters.
Can you guess the meanings of these words?

Another fact about Russian

One of the things that may make Russian sound strange at first is the way it combines letters that we do not use together in English:
e.g. the sounds S K V in **Москва**
We call these groups of letters *consonant clusters*.

K See if you can identify the consonant clusters in these words. Listen to the tape, then write down, using Roman letters, the three consonants that are grouped together in each word. The first one is done for you.
1 SKV

In this unit, we have not tried to teach you the Russian language, but rather to look at some ways in which it differs from English and consider why it perhaps sounds difficult to an unaccustomed ear.
To test how much you have learnt about Russian, complete Exercise L.

МОСКОВСКИЙ ГОСУДАРСТВЕННЫЙ

ЦИРК
на ленинских горах

ПЕРВЫЙ РАЗ – В ПЕРВЫЙ КЛАСС!

5.4
Конец дороги
для автомобилей

Извещение   Индекс
17/2

Поручение   Портье

Комната
Room *730*

Проживание с ——— по
Staying from

Предъявите при получении ключа
When you pick up your key please
show this card

HOTEL
Intourist
Moscow
Серия ТГ

ГОСУДАРСТВЕННЫЕ МУЗЕИ МОСКОВСКОГО КРЕМЛЯ МИНИСТЕРСТВА КУЛЬТУРЫ СССР

БИЛЕТ № 019758 ❄

Серия АЖ

На посещени
ГОСУДАРСТВЕН
ОРУЖЕЙНОЙ ПЛАТ
действителен тольк
НА 29 СЕНТЯБРЯ 1987 г
Начало сеанса в 12 ча
Вход через БОРОВИЦКИ

Цена 1 рубль

МОСКОВСКИЙ АКАДЕМИЧЕСКИЙ
ордена трудового красного знамени
ТЕАТР имени ВЛ. МАЯКОВСКОГО

Балкон 1 яруса

СЕРЕДИНА

РЯД 2 МЕСТО 24
Цена 2 р. 80 к.

Б/кн. № 000041 ❄

В Е Ч Е Р

Главное управление культуры исполкома Моссовета

Серия ТГ

МОСКОВСКИЙ АКАДЕМИЧЕСКИЙ
ордена трудового красного знамени
ТЕАТР имени ВЛ. МАЯКОВСКОГО

Балкон 1 яруса

СЕРЕДИНА

Б/кн. № 00004   п 2 МЕСТО 25

В Е Ч 1988 год 80 к.

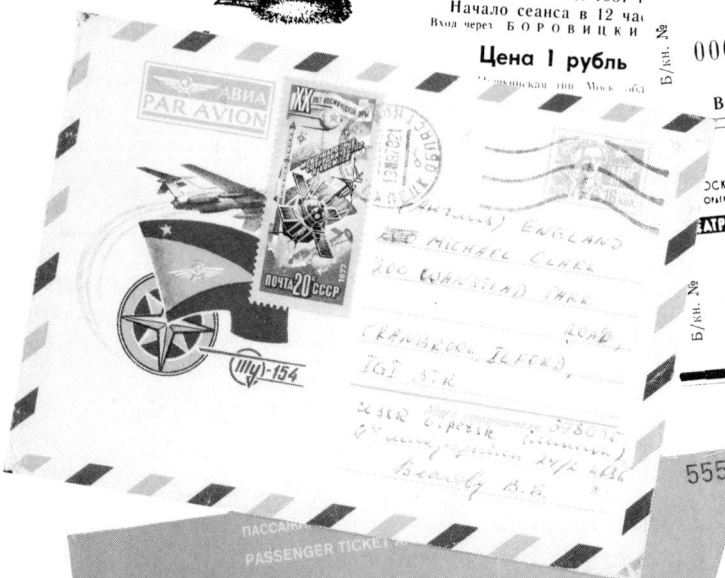

АВИА
PAR AVION

ПОЧТА 20к СССР

(England) ENGLAND

MICHAEL CLARK

555 4

ПАССАЖ

PASSENGER TICKET

АЭРОФЛОТ *Soviet airlines*

37, LENINGRADSKY PROSPEKT, MOSCOW, USSR

L True or false? Read these statements and say whether they are true or false.

1 Russian has fewer letters than English.
2 Vowels in Russian can be either hard or soft.
3 You cannot pronounce groups of consonants such as C K B together in Russian.
4 The letter **Ю** is pronounced 'yoo'.
5 The Russian letter **C** is pronounced the same as the Roman letter C.
6 The sound **Ц** exists in the Roman alphabet.
7 **да** means 'yes'.
8 The name for the Russian alphabet is the Cyrillic alphabet.
9 **футбол** is the Russian for 'football'.
10 This is the name of a town in Russia: **Лондон** .

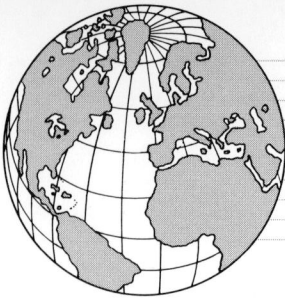

8 South Asian Languages

SOUTH ASIA: BACKGROUND INFORMATION

The Land

South Asia (the Indian sub-continent) consists of nearly one and three-quarter million square miles of land – ten per cent of the continent of Asia. The countries of South Asia are India, Pakistan, Bangladesh, Sri Lanka, Nepal and Bhutan. The land is very varied and can be divided into four main physical areas:
- the northern mountain zone (Himalayas and other mountain ranges)
- the Indo-Gangetic Plain (where the huge Indus and Ganges rivers flow)
- the desert area
- the Southern Peninsula and islands.

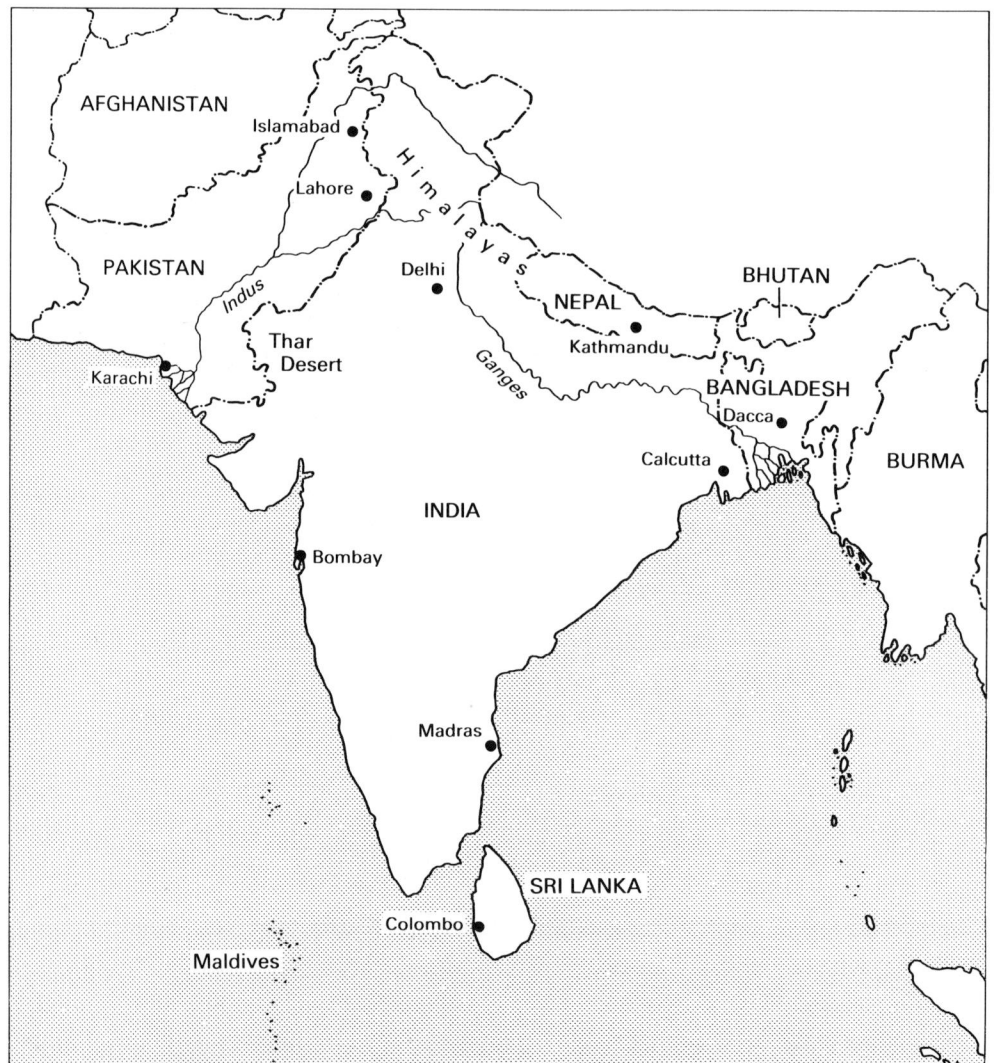

The History of South Asia

This area was the seat of a very ancient civilization. Between 500 BC and 1200 AD in particular, this civilization had great influence over the rest of the world. It is an area rich in jewels, spices, silks and other valuables and was therefore attractive to European traders and explorers.

India was a British colony from the eighteenth century until 1947 when it became independent. The original territory was divided to form what is present-day India, Pakistan (previously West Pakistan) and Bangladesh (previously East Pakistan). This was a convenient solution to the religious friction that existed in the original India, as most Muslims lived in the countries now known as Bangladesh and Pakistan and most Hindus lived in what is now India. However many families had no alternative but to move out of their homes into the areas where their co-religionists lived.

Indian painting from Rajasthan

South Asia has many natural resources including minerals and good farmland. Because these have not been sufficiently developed in the past, it has long been a very poor part of the world, with an extremely low standard of living. The governments of South Asian countries have for several years been working to overcome poverty by developing resources and improving farming techniques.

The People of South Asia

This is a very densely populated part of the world. More than about 850 million people live in India alone. Seventy-five per cent of the people live in rural villages and work on the land. The people of South Asia are followers of many different religions and include Hindus, Muslims, Buddhists, Christians and Sikhs.

Jain Temple, Calcutta, West Bengal

The Great Mosque, Lahore, Pakistan

The Languages of South Asia

Over one thousand different languages and dialects are spoken in South Asia. The languages of South Asia belong to two language families:

Dravidian	Indo-European
Tamil	Hindi, Nepali
Telugu	Urdu
	Bengali
	Gujarati
	Punjabi
	Sinhalese

Hindi is the official language of India, Urdu of Pakistan, Bengali of Bangladesh, and Sinhalese of Sri Lanka. The languages of South Asia use many different scripts. The scripts used for Hindi, Nepali, Bengali and Gujarati have come from ancient Sanskrit (the language used in Hindu holy scriptures). Urdu, however, uses Arabic script (the language of the holy book of Islam). Many people are familiar with more than one language.

Bengali	Gujarati	Hindi
বাংলা	અંગ્રેજ	हिंदी
Sinhalese	Tamil	Urdu
සිංහල	தமிழ்	اُردو زبان

A Copy these sentences into your books, filling in the missing word in each set. Can you add two more to each group?
1 Hindi, Urdu, Tamil, and Gujarati are all . . . . . . of South Asia.
2 Hinduism, Buddhism, Sikhism are all . . . . . . of South Asia.
3 Dacca, Delhi are . . . . . . in South Asia.
4 Bhutan, Nepal, Sri Lanka are all . . . . . . of South Asia.
5 Indus, Ganges are . . . . . . in South Asia.

B Name these South Asian languages:

1 தமிழ்	2 हिंदी	3 અંગ્રેજ
4 বাংলা	5 اُردو زبان	6 සිංහල

C Match the South Asian countries with their correct capitals

Countries	Capitals
Bangladesh	Katmandu
Bhutan	Colombo
India	Thimphu
Nepal	Islamabad
Pakistan	Dacca
Sri Lanka	Delhi

THE BENGALI LANGUAGE

Vishnu's Disk, fifth century, Patna, Bengal

Bengali is one of the main languages of South Asia. With 160 million, it is the language with the sixth largest number of speakers in the world. Bengali is the official language of Bangladesh and there are also speakers of Bengali in West Bengal and other Indian provinces such as Orissa, Bihar and Assam. While the majority of Bengali speakers are Muslim, there are many who follow other faiths such as Hindus, Buddhists, Christians and Sikhs. There are many thousands of Bengali speakers in Britain. Most of them originally came from the Sylhet region of Bangladesh.

Like Hindi, Bengali developed from the ancient language Sanskrit. If you compare Bengali script with Sanskrit and Hindi you can see the similarity.

Bengali	Hindi	Sanskrit
বাংলা	हिंदी	संस्कृतं

Bengali culture has a long and rich tradition, notably in painting, architecture, crafts, music and literature. The poet Rabindranath Tagore, who wrote in Bengali, won the Nobel prize for literature in 1913. His poetry is popular not only in Bangladesh, but in translation is greatly admired throughout the educated world.

Bangladesh: The Land

Eighty-five per cent of the land of Bangladesh consists of low, flat plains across which flow three great rivers: the Brahmaputra, the Ganges and the Meghna.

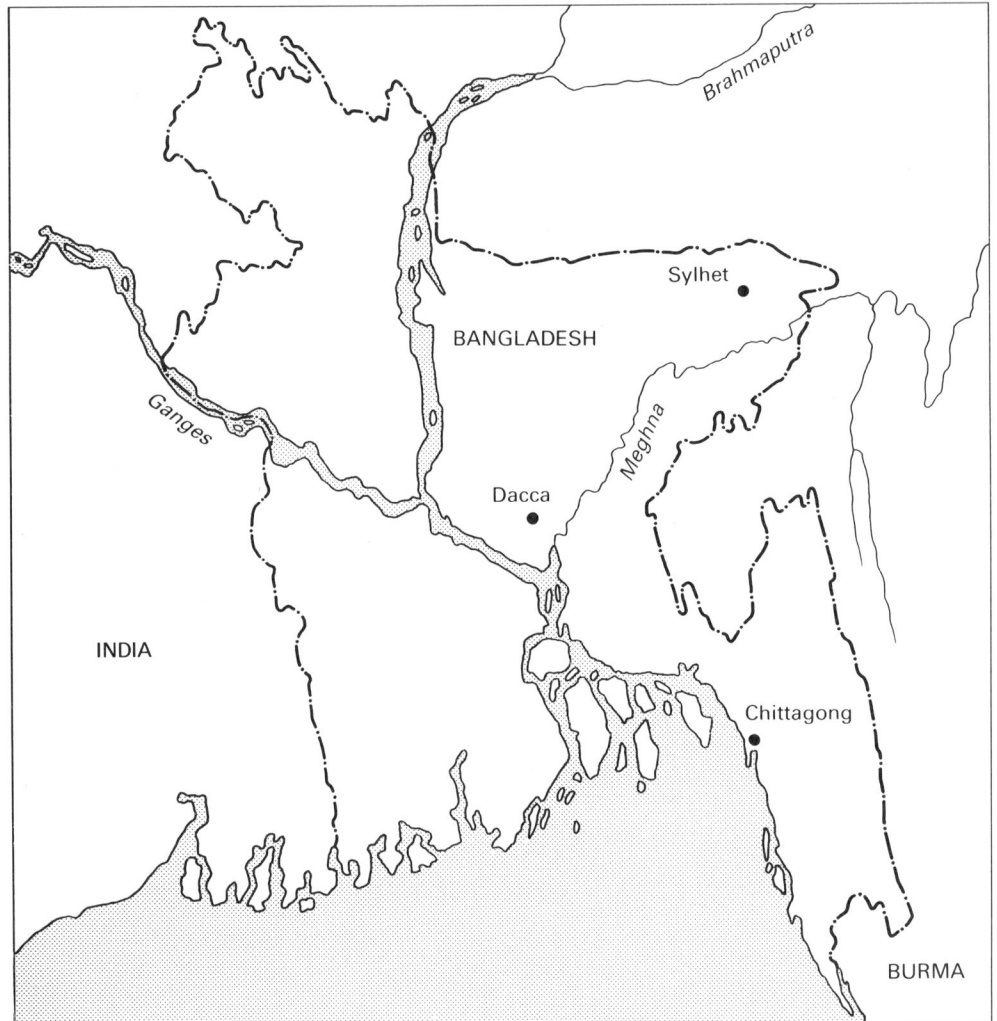

Many other smaller rivers, streams and canals flow through Bangladesh. The waterways are an important source of fish and also provide the chief means of transport in the country. The plains are full of fertile soil, left on the river banks after flooding. The climate is very hot and wet, with monsoon rains and storms frequently causing flooding on the low plains. Cyclones and tidal waves continue to cause much destruction and loss of life.

Eighty per cent of the people of Bangladesh farm the land. The fertile plains and the warm, humid climate are ideal for growing rice. Bangladesh is one of the leading rice-growing countries. Despite this, many people do not have enough to eat because of the high population and devastation by floods, cyclones and political turmoil.

The History of Bangladesh

Bangladesh was originally part of Bengal – a prosperous area ruled at different times by Hindu, Buddhist and Muslim leaders. The area became part of the British Empire in 1858 when Britain took control of India. Under British rule eastern Bengal (mostly a Muslim area) did not share the industrial development of western Bengal (where most people were Hindus). This led to conflict and rioting between Muslims and Hindus in Bengal.

In 1947, when India became independent, eastern Bengal became East Pakistan, part of the Muslim country of Pakistan whose official language was Urdu. The Bengali speakers of East Pakistan felt they had little in common with Urdu-speaking West Pakistan and eventually civil war broke out.

In 1971 East Pakistan became the independent nation of Bangladesh, with Bengali as its official language. Every year on 21st February, the nation celebrates Shaheed Day (Martyrs' Day) in memory of the 'language martyrs' who fought for the right to keep their Bengali language and culture.

D Match up the words below with the drawings underneath.
1 Brahmaputra
2 Dacca
3 Rabindranath Tagore
4 Sanskrit
5 Monsoon

a

b

c

d

राजा ॥ शकुन्तलां विलोक्य । आत्मगतम् ॥
किं नु खलु यथा वयमस्यामेवमियमप्यस्मान्प्रति स्यात् ।
अथवा लब्धावकाशा मे प्रार्थना । कुतः ।
e   वाचं न मिश्रयति यद्यपि मे वचोभिः

Learn some Bengali

You will hear how to pronounce these Bengali words and phrases from the cassette which accompanies this book.
To help you learn to speak and understand some Bengali, the words and phrases below have been 'transliterated' – that is written in Roman script rather than Bengali script.

Greetings

Bengali speakers usually use the Muslim (Arabic) greeting:

As-salam-alaikum

reply: **Walaikum-as-salam**

Names

Question:
Polite form (used with most adults)

Apnar nam ki? (What is your name?)

Familiar form (used with children/family)

Tomar nam ki? (What is your name?)

Answer:

Amar nam Mary. (My name is Mary)

Where you live

Question:
Polite form

Apni kothai thaken? (Where do you live?)

Familiar form

Tumi kothai thako? (Where do you live?)

Answer:

Ami Londoney thaki (I live in London)

Ami Leedsey thaki (I live in Leeds)

Ages

Question:
Polite form

Apnar boyosh koto? (How old are you?)

Familiar form

Tomar boyosh koto? (How old are you?)

Answer:

Amar boyosh baro (I am twelve)

Amar boyosh tero (I am thirteen)

Numbers

১	ek	1	৮	aat	8
২	dui	2	৯	noy	9
৩	tin	3	১০	dosh	10
৪	char	4	১১	egaro	11
৫	panch	5	১২	baro	12
৬	choy	6	১৩	tero	13
৭	shat	7	১৪	choudyo	14

The Bengali Alphabet

অ	আ	ই	ঈ	উ	ঊ
a	ā	i	ī	u	ū
ঋ	এ	ঐ	ও	ঔ	
ri	ē	ai	ō	au	

ক	খ	গ	ঘ	ঙ
ka	kha	ga	gha	nga
চ	ছ	জ	ঝ	ঞ
cha	caha	ja	jha	nya
ট	ঠ	ড	ঢ	ণ
ta	tha	pla	plha	na
ত	থ	দ	ধ	ন
ta	tha	da	dha	na
প	ফ	ব	ভ	ম
pa	pha	ba	bla	ma
য	র	ল	শ	ষ
ya	ra	la	sa	sha
স	হ	ড়	ঢ়	য়
sa	ha	ra	ra	za

ৎ	ং	ঃ	ঁ

You will need to listen to the tape with your teacher before trying the speaking and listening activities.

E 1 a Greet each other in Bengali.
   b Ask each other's names in Bengali.
   c Ask each other's ages in Bengali.
   d Ask where your partner lives.
 2 Point to each of the numbers below and ask your partner to say them in Bengali:

1	2	3	4	5	6	7
8	9	10	11	12	13	14

3 Pretend to be each of these people and say your name, age and where you live in Bengali. Listen to your partner doing the same.

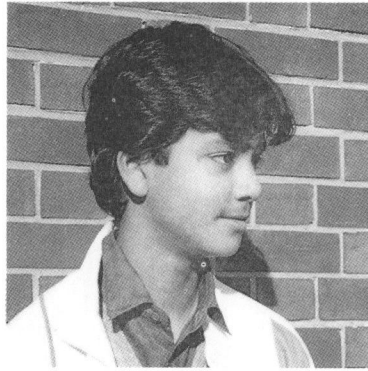

a Shakeel, 13, Birmingham

b Rosemary, 11, London

c Peter, 12, Bradford

d Mohammed, 14, Coventry

e Maria, 9, Peterborough

f Nagila, 10, Bedford

F 1 Listen to the tape and pick the correct English translation of what you hear.

a My name is Salih.
How old are you?
Greetings!

b What is your name?
My name is Mohammed.
My name is Rubeena.

c What is your name?
How old are you?
My name is Kiki.

d I live in London.
I am twelve.
I live in Sylhet.

e Where do you live?
What is your name?
How old are you?

f I am eleven.
I am twelve.
I am thirteen.

2 Write as figures the numbers you hear on the tape.

3 Answer briefly in English (one word answers are sufficient) the three questions you hear on the tape.

G

1 Practise writing the Bengali figures for the numbers 1–14.
2 Read these sentences about people's ages and find out how old each one is.

a আমার বয়স ১০

b আমার বয়স ৯

c আমার বয়স ১২

d আমার বয়স ১৪

3 Practise writing the words for 'Bangladesh' (Bangla = Bengali, Desh = country) and 'Bengali Language' (Bangla Bhasha).
Bangladesh

বাংলাদেশ

Bengali Language

বাংলা ভাষা

4 Read this passage of Bengali about a boy called Mujid. Then answer the questions below.

আমার নাম মুজিব। আমার বয়স ১৩।

আমি বাংলা ভাষা বলি।

আমি বাংলাদেশে থাকি।

a How old is Mujib?
b What language does he speak?
c Where does he live?

9 Bahasa Indonesia

THE COUNTRY

Indonesia is a country composed of a stretch of islands lying across the Equator to the extreme south of the Asian land-mass.

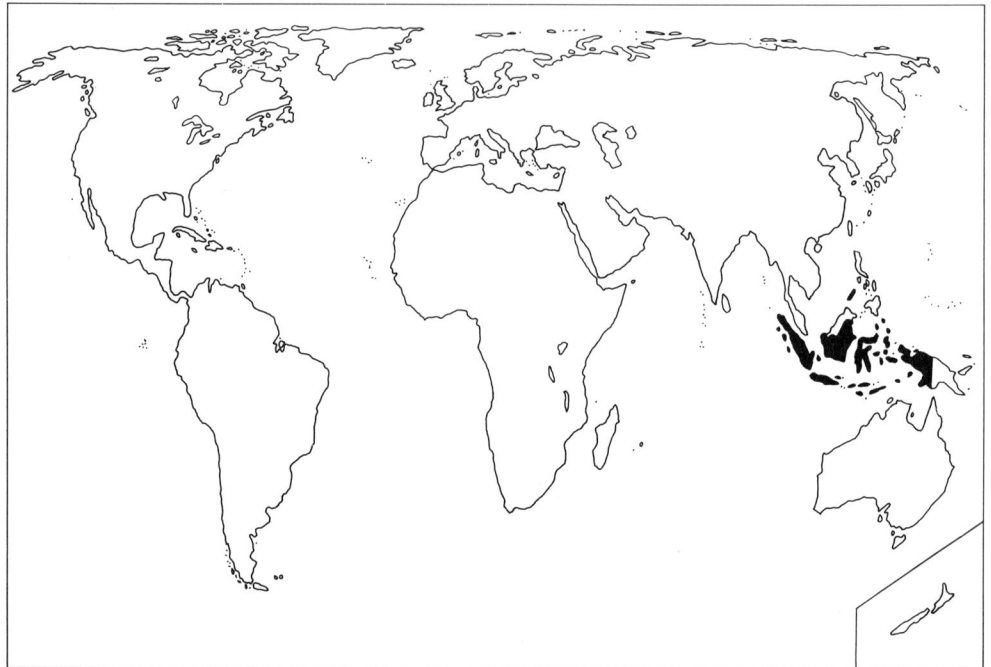

There are over 13,500 islands in Indonesia. Under 1,000 are permanently inhabited and only about half have been named. Five of the ten largest islands in the world are in Indonesia. The Indonesians count the seas around their islands as part of their country and call it **Taneh Air Kita** or 'Our Land and Water'. The total land and sea area is five million square kilometres.

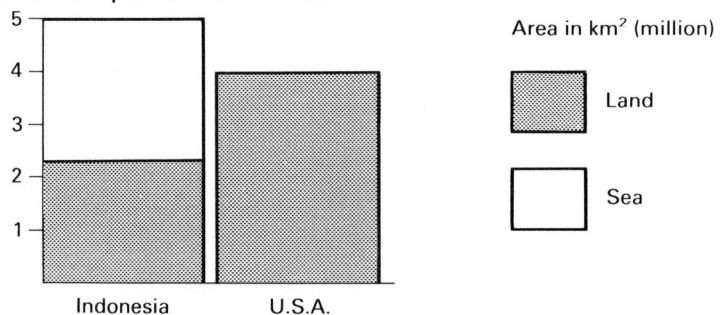

Area in km² (million)

Land

Sea

Indonesia is a land of contrasts; coastal mangrove forests, tall evergreen tropical rain forests, swamps and lagoons, terraced rice fields and rubber plantations. Indonesia has more than 400 volcanos,

Terraces of flooded rice paddies, Bali

Mount Merapi, Java

lying as it does within the 'Ring of Fire'. Only between seventy and eighty are still active although there are still ten major earthquakes on average every year and about three minor tremors are registered every day.

The volcanic soil is very fertile. With the very hot and wet equatorial climate, as many as three rice crops can be grown a year in some parts of the country. Even the slopes of the volcanos are planted by using a system of terraces.

A Use your Atlas to find the names of the five largest islands in Indonesia.

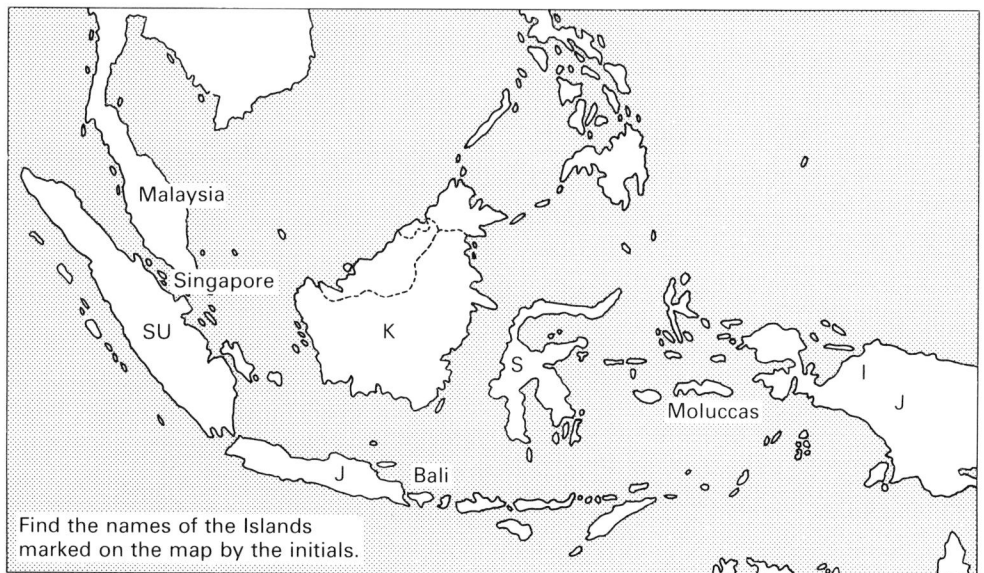

Find the names of the Islands marked on the map by the initials.

Indonesia, Malaysia and Singapore

Language and People

The population of Indonesia is ethnically very diverse.

Two girls from Bali

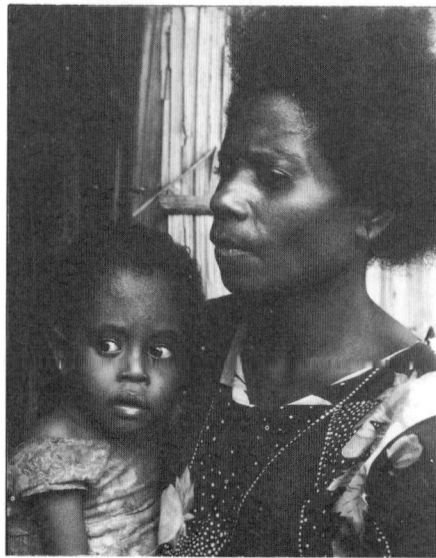

Mother and child, West Irian

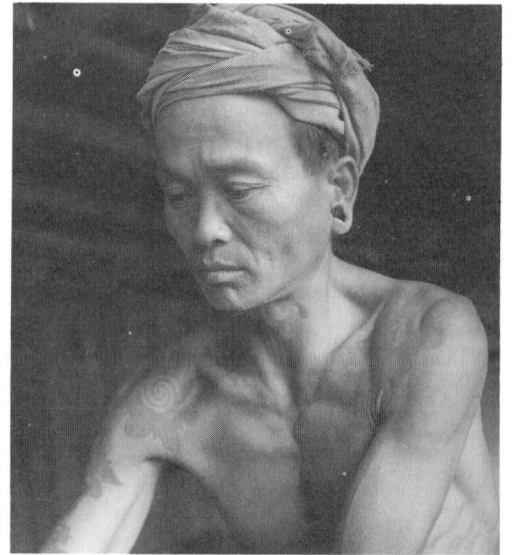

Dyak tribesman, Borneo

Although Bahasa Indonesia is the national language of over 140 million speakers and everyone learns it at school, beginning in the third year of primary school, it is only the second or even the third language for the majority of Indonesians. Bahasa Indonesia belongs to the *Austronesian* family of languages, having developed from Malay which was one of approximately 350 languages spoken within the region.

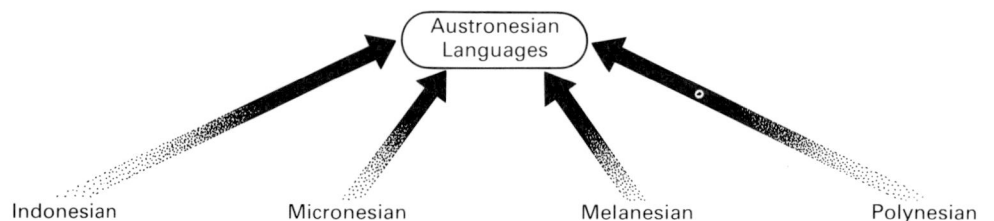

Austronesian Languages

Indonesian   Micronesian   Melanesian   Polynesian

Among the other languages still spoken in Indonesia are Javanese, Balinese, Batak and Sundanese.

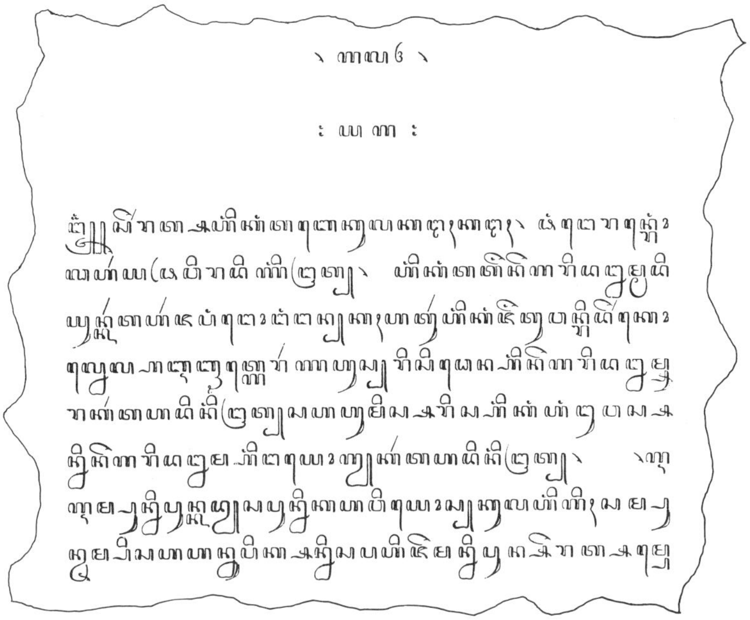

Javanese script.

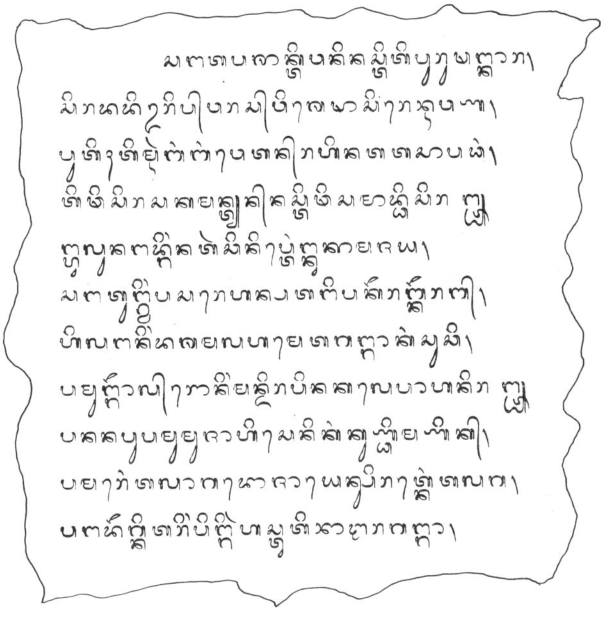

Balinese script

Batak script

Ninety per cent of Indonesians are Muslim and so Arabic is the liturgical language of most Indonesians.

The opening of the Holy Qur'an

In the name of Allāh, the Beneficent, the Merciful.

بِسْمِ اللهِ الرَّحْمٰنِ الرَّحِيْمِ ۟

1 Praise be to Allāh, the Lord of the worlds,

اَلْحَمْدُ لِلّٰهِ رَبِّ الْعٰلَمِيْنَ ۙ

2 The Beneficent, the Merciful,

الرَّحْمٰنِ الرَّحِيْمِ ۙ

3 Master of the day of Requital.

مٰلِكِ يَوْمِ الدِّيْنِ ۗ

4 Thee do we serve and Thee do we beseech for help.

اِيَّاكَ نَعْبُدُ وَاِيَّاكَ نَسْتَعِيْنُ ۗ

5 Guide us on the right path,

اِهْدِنَا الصِّرَاطَ الْمُسْتَقِيْمَ ۙ

6 The path of those upon whom Thou hast bestowed favours,

صِرَاطَ الَّذِيْنَ اَنْعَمْتَ عَلَيْهِمْ ۙ غَيْرِ

7 Not those upon whom wrath is brought down, nor those who go astray.

الْمَغْضُوْبِ عَلَيْهِمْ وَلَا الضَّآلِّيْنَ ۟

Bahasa Indonesia acts as a unifying force, the need for which is recognised in the country's coat of arms. Its motto '**Bhinneka Tunggal Ika**' means 'We are many but we are one'.

HISTORY

This part of South East Asia has been subject to wave after wave of migrations and invasions. Indians, Arabs, Chinese, Melanesians and later British, Portuguese, Dutch and Japanese have all settled at one time or another in Indonesia.

The islands which now form Indonesia were never considered as one territory until after the arrival of Dutch traders in 1596. The Dutch gained control of the area, helped by the fighting between rival sultans, and ruled it for 350 years under the name of 'Dutch East Indies'.

A number of Nationalist movements working for independence sprang up at the beginning of the twentieth century. The Pan Indonesia Youth Conference of 1928 adopted Bahasa Indonesia as the national language. It was to be promoted as an important part of the fight for freedom from Dutch domination. Finally, after considerable bloodshed, Indonesia became independent in December 1948.

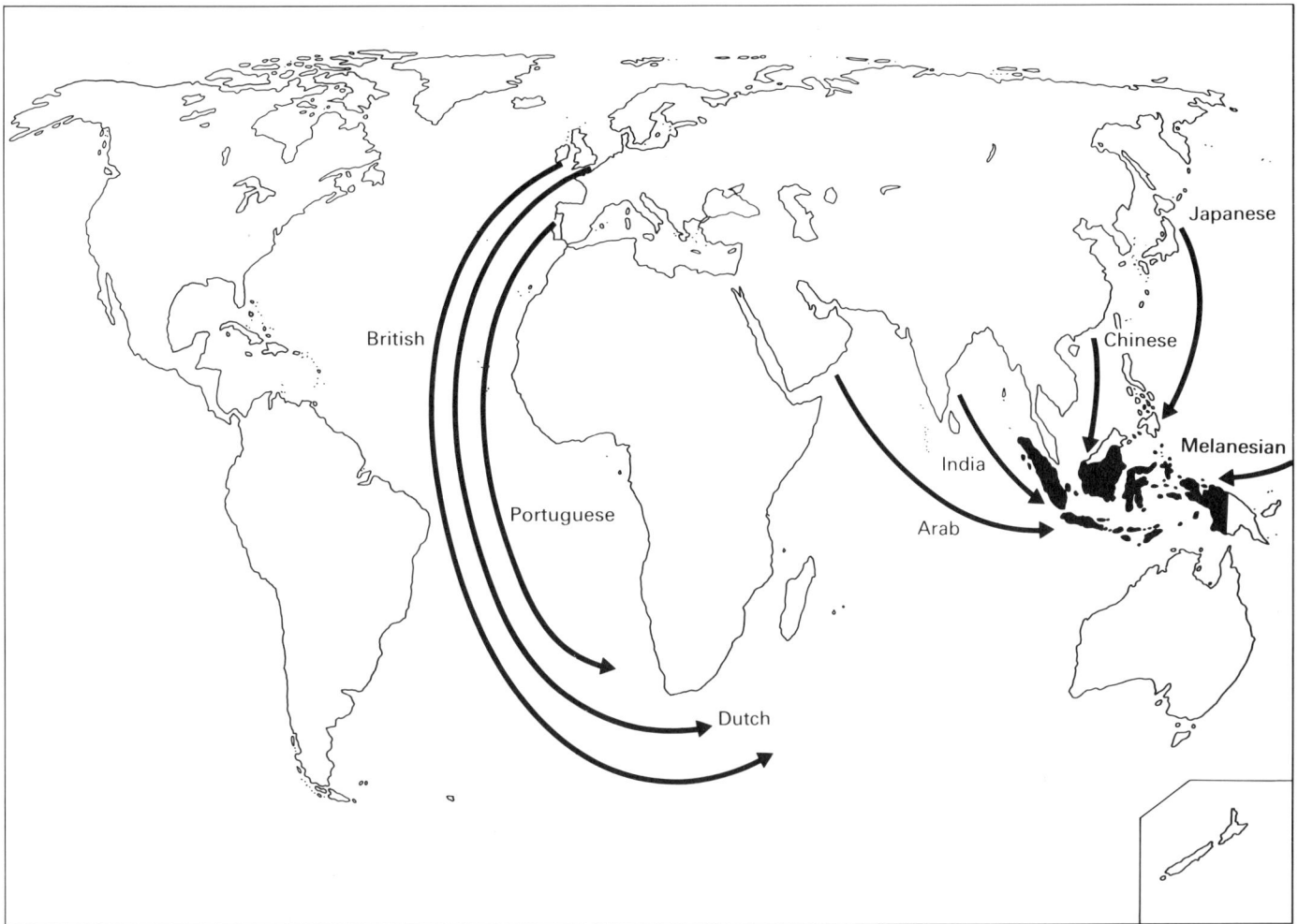

Invasions of the islands now forming the territory of Indonesia

---

B 1 Does Bahasa mean 'language' or 'southern'?
2 How many of the world's ten largest islands are in Indonesia? Can you name them?
3 About how many of the 13,677 islands have been named? Approximately one quarter, a half, or three-quarters?
4 Does '**Taneh Air Kita**' mean 'Our Land and Water', or 'Our Islands'?
5 What language do most Indonesians use for prayer?
6 Is Bahasa Indonesia the mother tongue for the majority or the minority of Indonesians?
7 About how many other languages are spoken in Indonesia?
8 Complete these sentences:
  a In 1596 . . .
  b In 1928 . . .
  c In 1948 . . .

Wordfinder

If you use every letter in the wordfinder you can get the answers to the following clues:

ACROSS:
Three islands in Indonesia.
The sister language to Bahasa Indonesia.
A volcano off the west coast of Java.
The capital.
The religion of 90% of Indonesians.
A people ruling the area for 350 years.
The words for a) water; b) bus; c) speech.

DOWN:
Another three islands in Indonesia.
Another volcano.
The name of the traders who brought Islam to the area.
A forbidden food for Muslims.

UP:
A language spoken in Sumatra.

BACK:
The continent in which Indonesia lies.

I	R	I	A	N	J	A	Y	A	K	A
B	A	S	C	S	A	D	U	T	C	H
D	R	U	E	U	V	F	A	I	S	A
K	A	L	I	M	A	N	T	A	N	M
A	B	A	H	A	S	A	A	I	R	E
T	S	W	G	T	M	A	L	A	Y	R
A	H	E	K	R	A	K	A	T	O	A
B	I	S	J	A	K	A	R	T	A	P
I	J	I	S	L	A	M	B	A	L	I

THE LANGUAGE

Nouns

Bahasa Indonesia has borrowed words widely from the other indigenous languages of the area and also from the languages spoken by successive waves of people who invaded the islands. Since 1975, about half the new words that have entered the language are from English and these recent borrowings have generally not even changed their spelling. They show the increasing influence of western life. We find that large numbers deal with the media, entertainment and business such as *bandleader*, *budget*, *businessman* and *box office*.

There are many other words that have been in common use in Bahasa Indonesia or Malay for much longer. You will also be able to recognise them quite easily, although many of these older borrowings from Dutch or English show some change in spelling and sometimes their pronunciation has also altered.

D See if you can guess these:

1 **Nopember**		4 **pinsil**
2 **pos**		5 **asisten**
3 **pena**		

E Now listen to the tape and see if you can match the words you hear with the correct picture. Make a list *a–l* first so that you can write down the number for each one.

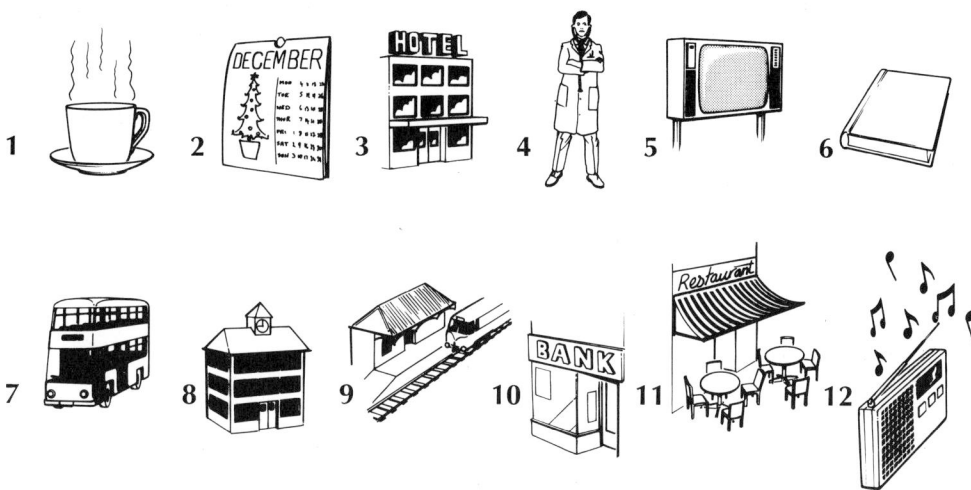

F Now try some more. Make a list in your book, matching the words below with the correct illustrations.

kopi   kelinik   trapel   cek   mobil   amplop   setuden

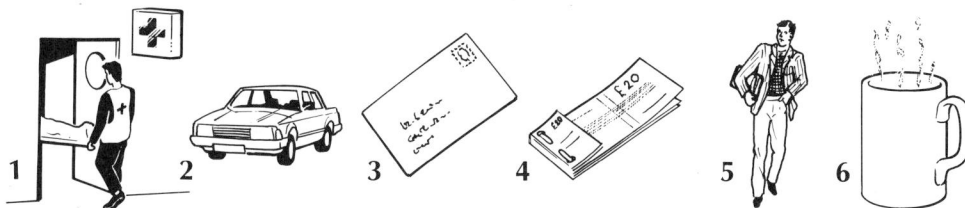

Have another look at the words and say the original English. What sound do you think a written '**k**' represents? What about a '**c**'? Can you describe what the words '**kelinik**' and '**setuden**' have in common, regarding the way their sound has changed?

G Now play the tape again for exercise E and the words used in exercise F several times to train your ear, so that you can go on and read the following words to yourself. Write them down and put the correct English next to each.

telepon   konsert   taksi   coklat   gelas   bir   nama   polisi   turis   rumah

Batak house

Aerial view of typical village, Sumatra

Komodo village, Nusa Tenggara

When you look at pictures of Indonesian houses in the countryside it is easy to see why the word **rumah** means house rather than 'room'. Houses are often just a single big room where bedding can be laid out at night and where you can sit in the shade in the day. In hot countries people do not need to spend so much time indoors. Cooking, washing and washing-up are often performed out-of-doors, and many more social gatherings can take place in the open air than in cold countries.

We call words like **rumah** and room 'false friends' because they look as though they have the same meaning but really mean something different. You will even find them in different varieties of the same language. For example, 'suspenders' hold up your stockings in the UK but they hold up your trousers in the USA where 'braces' are for straightening teeth!

Although people do spend a lot ot time outside, we must not forget that Indonesia lies on the Equator. The average rainfall of 180 centimetres shows that when it rains it can really pour, but although the rain may be heavy it is often quite warm. When the sun comes out it is hot enough to dry you and your clothes off in no time at all! As you can see, this school boy does not seem to be any the worse for his soaking.

Satu Setuden

Now look at the picture below of a class of hardworking students in a village school in Sumatra and you will see that the titles of both pictures use the word **setuden** even though in one picture there is one student and in the other there are several student**s**.

Tujuh Setuden

School children hard at work in a village school, Sumatra

Plurals

When it is obvious that you are talking about more than one person or thing, as in this case where the number 'two' is used, you do not need to change the *noun*. When it is not obvious, then the word is repeated twice.

pena    dua pena    penapena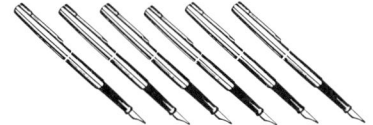

This tourist forgot all about how *plurals* are formed in Indonesia and got into rather a mess!

"Taksi! Taksi!"

Repeating the word may be easy enough when you are speaking but could make even quite simple sentences a bit long and tiring to write. Consequently, the Indonesians generally use a quick and efficient way of showing plurals in written form:

mobil   mobil2

Numbers

Indonesian numbers are very easy to form and as we have seen do not need a *plural noun*.

H Listen to some Indonesian numbers.

The first series was 1–14. The second was 10, 20, 30, 40 and so on up to 100. Here they are written down for you to learn. Listen to them again and read them at the same time.

1	**satu**	8	**delapan**
2	**dua**	9	**sembilan**
3	**tiga**	10	**sepuluh**
4	**empat**	11	**sebelas**
5	**lima**	12	**dua belas**
6	**enam**	13	**tiga belas**
7	**tujuh**	14	**empat belas** and so on

20	**dua pulah**
30	**tiga pulah**
40	**empat pulah** and so on
100	**seratus**

I Write down the following in English:

1	**tiga**	7	**lima puluh**
2	**delapan**	8	**sembilan**
3	**satu**	9	**empat buku**
4	**dua belas**	10	**enam kopi**
5	**lima**	11	**tujah bis**
6	**sepuluh**	12	**seratus pena**

J Now that you know the low numbers quite well, see if you can recognise some high numbers. Listen to the twelve numbers on the tape and write them down.

K You are going to hear five more numbers. First of all write them down in figures and when you are sure you have the correct numbers write them out in words.

Possessive adjectives

We are going to continue using some simple *nouns* in Bahasa Indonesia. In conversations it is often very important to know exactly who is the owner of an object or what family or group a person belongs to.

"This is *my* chocolate, it doesn't belong to my friends. It is not *his* and it doesn't belong to *her* either."

We call words like 'my', 'his', 'her' *possessive adjectives* because they describe things or people showing who possesses or owns them.

rumah saya   **rumah saudara**   **rumah mereka**

rumahnya   **rumanya**

All these people are explaining to whom the house belongs. *My, your* and *their* are separate words but *his* and *her* are different because they are attached to the end of the word 'house'. We call this a *suffix* from two words in Latin (**sub** meaning 'under' and **fingere** meaning 'to fix'). You can find out a lot more about suffixes in Unit Ten.

We also see that the same suffix **-nya** is used for both 'his' and 'her', and many languages do not make a distinction because it is usually quite easy in a conversation to tell which is meant. Look at the previous pictures again and see if they are clear.

Sometimes Bahasa Indonesia makes distinctions that we do not have in English. For example, there are two different words for 'our' whereas English uses one word for all situations. When 'our' includes the listener the word is **kita** and when it does not include him **kami** is used.

rumah kita   **rumah kami**

L Write these phrases down and put the English next to them:

1 **kelinik mereka**
2 **mobil saya**
3 **bukunya**
4 **doktor kita**
5 **teh saudara**

6 **coklat saya**
7 **trapel cek2 mereka**
8 **namanya**
9 **musik kami**
10 **kopinya**

M Look at the pictures and choose the correct decription for each:

**rumah saya   koklat kita   bank saudara   tehnya   mobil kami   taksinya
setuden saya   TV saudara**

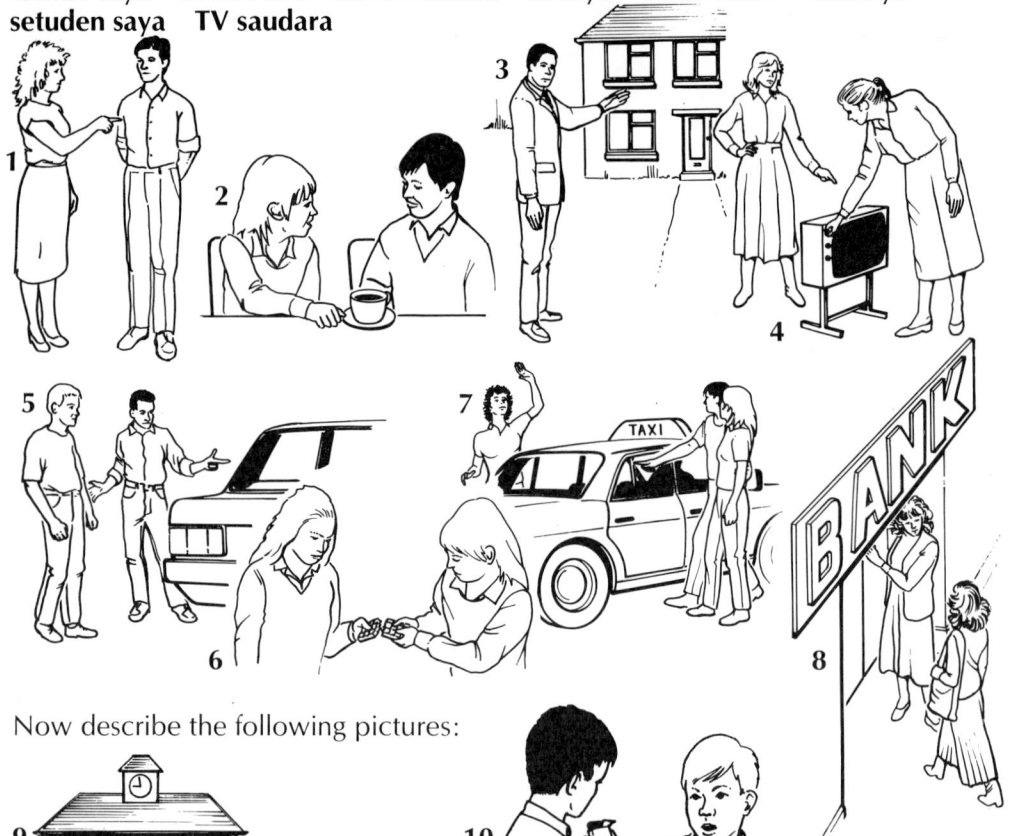

Now describe the following pictures:

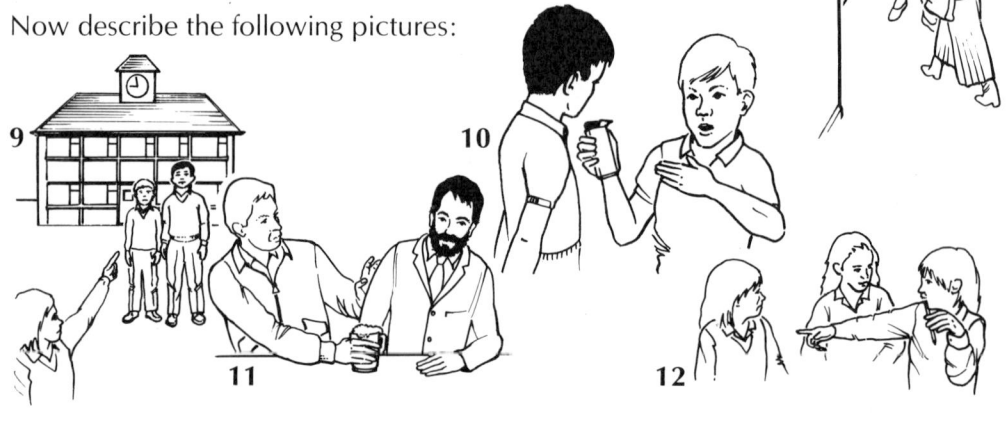

Pronouns

It is very important to Indonesians to show proper respect for status and position. The educated speaker of Bahasa Indonesia will use eight to ten different ways of saying 'you' depending on the social position and age of the person he or she is talking to. This may seem complicated but is much simpler than the situation in Old Malay from which Bahasa developed and the distinctions in status in Javanese are even more finely graded.

Even a visitor to the country needs to use several different forms of 'you' to avoid giving offence. We have already met one of them: **saudara** as well as meaning 'your' is also used as the *pronoun* 'you' in fairly formal situations between two adults who are on roughly equal terms (for example, when your parents go to school to discuss your work with the teacher). It is not, however, used between friends. Nor would it be correct to use it to someone more important or in a superior position since it would sound too familiar.

Bapak which shortens to **Pak**   you/sir/father
Ibu which shortens to **Bu**   you/madam/mother

As you can see both these imply respect and must be used to older people or people in positions of authority, such as your headteacher.

Saudara fairly formal between adults of equal status
Awa between friends
Kamu adult speaking to child

Some Indonesians feel that it would be preferable to have a general 'you' for everyone. At one time **saudara** was suggested, and an attempt has been made to use **anda** but neither have met with much success as a pronoun covering all situations. However **anda** has been added to the long list of 'you' pronouns and is now the usual way of showing 'you' in advertisements.

N Select from this list the word for 'you' which would be appropriate in the following situations:

Pak Ibu Saudara Awa Kamu Anda

1 When you are speaking to your teacher.
2 When you are talking to your friends.
3 When you are being urged to try a new soap powder.
4 When your headmaster is talking to you.
5 When your teacher is discussing you with another member of staff.
6 When you are talking to the headmistress.

We have not yet looked at any *verbs* or actions in Bahasa Indonesia. Here are some common ones:

beli	to buy
datang	to come
sampai	to arrive
makan	to eat
minum	to drink
masak	to cook
tidur	to sleep
mandi	to have a bath

The big earthenware jar that holds the water for your shower is also called **mandi**.

You can see that none of these are at all like their English equivalents. There are not nearly so many borrowed *verbs* in Bahasa Indonesia so guesswork is not much use to us here. However, verbs are very easy to use: the correct *pronoun* shows who is doing the action and there is no need to *conjugate* (change the endings). You already know several pronouns for 'you' and just like **saudara** most of the others are the same as the possesive adjectives. For example:

rumah saya my house   **rumah mereka** their house
saya makan I eat   **mereka makan** they eat
dia makan coklat she/he is eating chocolate
but,
coklatnya his/her chocolate

O Write down the English for the following actions:

1 saya minum
2 saudara makan
3 kami beli
4 mereka masak
5 dia sampai

6 mereka mandi
7 Pak tidur
8 dia datang
9 Bu beli coklat

Finally one with a new noun for you to guess:

10 Saya makan di (in) rumah makan

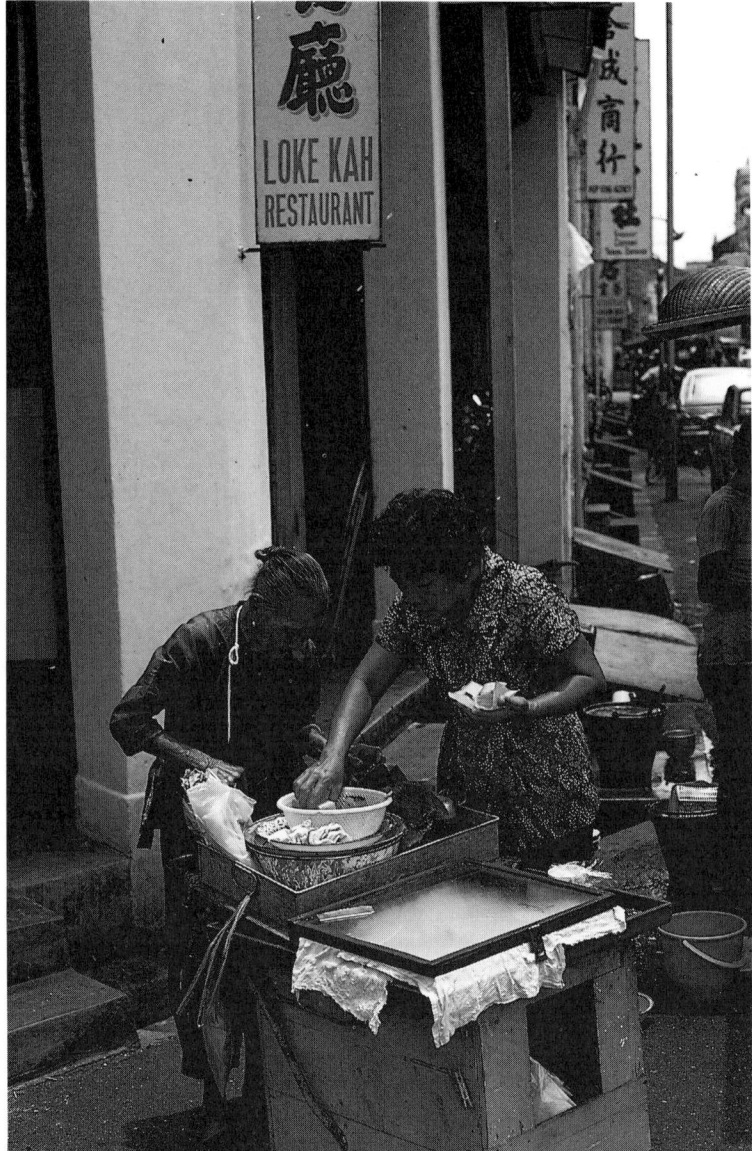

Rumah makan

The picture above shows a **rumah makan**, a simple eating place of which there are very many in Indonesia. Should you prefer something a little more sophisticated, the **restoran** with its 'borrowed' name is on a grander scale with correspondingly much higher prices. However, you may eat better at the more traditional restaurant if you choose your menu carefully!

P We are now ready to read some complete sentences. Use the vocabulary at the end of this unit to help you. Match up the Bahasa Indonesia and the English:

1	Dia makan coklat.	**a**	You are drinking tea.
2	Saudara minum teh.	**b**	We are buying a book.
3	Saya tidak beli buku.	**c**	They are eating chocolate.
4	Dia beli pena2.	**d**	You are not drinking tea.
5	Kita beli buku.	**e**	I am sleeping.
6	Pak tidur.	**f**	He is buying pens.
7	Mereka makan coklat.	**g**	I am not buying a book.
8	Saya tidur.	**h**	She is eating chocolate.
9	Mereka beli pena2.	**i**	You are sleeping.
10	Saudara tidak minum teh.	**j**	They are buying pens.

Questions and negatives

You will have noticed that two of the sentences in exercise P were about people 'not' performing an action.

Here are two more negative sentences:

Saya *tidak* **datang.**	I am not coming.
Bu *tidak* **tidur.**	You are not sleeping.

The 'negative' **tidak** goes between the *pronoun* and the *verb*.

It is also very easy to form questions in Bahasa Indonesia. The word **apakah** at the beginning of a sentence turns it into a question and there is no need to make any other changes.

Dia minum kopi.	She drinks coffee.
Apakah dia minum kopi?	Does she drink coffee?

Of course you can use both these words together:

Kamu tidur.	**Apakah kamu tidak tidur?**
You are asleep.	Aren't you asleep?

Q How would you say that the following are not happening?:

1	Saya datang.	4	Kita makan.
2	Pak minum teh.	5	Dia beli pena2.
3	Mereka mandi.	6	Saudara tidur.

Now turn them into questions.

R Choose the correct question to go with each situation:

1 **Apakah dia mandi?**
2 **Apakah kita makan?**
3 **Apakah dia beli buku?**
4 **Apakah mereka tidak datang?**
5 **apakah Bu tidur?**

a You are asking your mother what your sister is doing.
b You want to know if your headmistress has gone to buy the new text book.
c You want to know if your friends are going to pick you up or not.
d You want to know if lunch is ready.
e You want to find out if your teacher is really asleep.

S You can now write some sentences in Bahasa Indonesia:

1 I drink.	**5** You are not eating.
2 He doesn't cook.	**6** Isn't she buying a car?
3 We sleep.	**7** They don't drink beer.
4 Do they buy chocolate?	**8** Is she having a bath?

We have already seen that there is no need to change the endings of verbs (*conjugate*) in Bahasa Indonesia: the pronouns show quite clearly *who* is doing the action. There is also no need to make a change to show *when* an action takes place. *Tense* is usually made clear by some reference to the time. The most straight forward way is by showing on which day *it happened, is happening* or *will happen*.

---

kemarin	yesterday	
semalam	last night	so
besok	tomorrow	
Saya sampai *besok*		I will come tomorrow
Saya sampai *kemarin*		I came yesterday
Saya sampai *semalam*		I came last night

Bahasa Indonesia is quite different from English in how it shows time (*tense*) since in English the verb has to change. Chinese is another language in which people manage quite easily without altering the verbs to make tenses.

T Write the English for the following:

1 Dia makan besok.
2 Saya minum semalam.
3 Mereka tidak beli coklat kemarin.
4 Apakah saudara sampai besok?
5 Kita mandi semalam.
6 Apakah Pak tidur kemarin?
7 Saya tidak masak kemarin.
8 Apakah Bu tidak datang besok?

U Now write the Bahasa Indonesia for these sentences:

1 They are arriving tomorrow.
2 We didn't buy any tea yesterday.
3 Did he arrive last night?
4 They are not going to buy a car tomorrow.
5 I had a bath last night.
6 Didn't she come yesterday?
7 I will eat some chocolate tomorrow.
8 Didn't you sleep well last night?

Sometimes it is necessary to give more information than just the day that the action occurs. Bahasa Indonesia does this by using what are known as *tense markers* and places them before the verb.

future	**akan**	will
past	**sudah**	already
	belum	not yet
	baru	recently, to have just
present	**sedang**	is . . . . . ing
	masih	still
so		
	Saya *masih* **makan**	I am still eating
	Saya *belum* **makan**	I have not yet eaten
	Saya *akan* **makan**	I will eat

V Write the English for these sentences:

1 **Saya sudah minum**
2 **Mereka akan tidur.**
3 **Bu masih minum.**
4 **Kita baru beli mobil.**

5 **Dia sampai besok.**
6 **Pak belum beli pinsil2.**
7 **Saya minum teh semalam.**
8 **Dia sedang mandi.**

Here are some new words that would be very useful to you in Indonesia.

nasi rice
ayam chicken
guru teacher

Two important *prepositions*: **ke** to
di at, in

and a *conjunction*: **dan** and

to help you with more complex sentences.
For example:
Guru saya makan nasi di restoran semalam.
My teacher ate rice in the restaurant last night.

Saya datang ke restoran besok. Saya akan makan ayam dan nasi.
I will come to the restaurant tomorrow. I will eat chicken and rice.

You will see that by using these and all the work you have done so far you can already understand quite complicated sentences and even say quite a lot in Bahasa Indonesia.

W Write the English for the following:

1 **Saya sudah minum teh.**
2 **Dua taksi baru datang.**
3 **Dia belum sampai.**
4 **Setuden2 tidak tidur semalam.**
5 **Apakah Pak akan minum kopi?**

Now the Bahasa Indonesia for these:

6 I will come to your house tomorrow.
7 We have not yet eaten the chicken.
8 They are still having a bath.
9 He cooked rice last night.
10 Have you recently bought a car?

X Now translate these longer sentences:

1 Gurunya baru beli pena2 dan dua buku.
2 Empat turis tidur di hotel besok.
3 Apakah dua doctor datang ke sekolah kemarin?
4 Bapak saya sedang beli seratus buku.
5 Mereka akan sampai ke setasiun.
6 Saya belum datang ke pos.
7 Mereka minum kopi dan makan nasi.
8 Apakah guru mereka sudah datang ke bank?
9 Kita minum koklat di rumah makan.
10 Polisi2 baru sampai ke setasiun.

11 My teacher is buying some chocolate at the station.
12 Will they go to the concert tomorrow?
13 My mother has just cooked the chickens.
14 We didn't sleep in the house last night.
15 He has already drunk five glasses of beer.

VOCABULARY

Nouns

air	water	nama	name
amplop	envelope	nasi	rice
asisten	assistant	Nopember	November
ayam	chicken	pena	pen
Bahasa	speech	pensil	pencil
bank	bank	polisi	police
bir	beer	pos	post (office)
bis	bus	restoran	restaurant
buku	book	rumah	house
coklat	chocolate	rumah makan	simple restaurant
Desember	December	sekolah	school
doktor	doctor	setasiun	station
gelas	glass	setuden	student
guru	teacher	taksi	taxi
kelinik	clinic	taneh	land
konsert	concert	teh	tea
kopi	coffee	telepon	telephone
mandi	jar for water	trapel cek	traveller's cheque
mobil	car	turis	tourist
musik	music	TV	television

Numerals

satu	1	tujuh	7
dua	2	delapan	8
tiga	3	sembilan	9
empat	4	sepuluh	10
lima	5	sebelas	11
enam	6	seratus	100

Subject pronouns		
	anda	you (used in advertisements)
	awa	you (used between friends)
	bapak	you (to an older/more important man)
	bu	you (to an older/more important woman)
	dia	he/she
	ibu	you (to an older/more important woman)
	kami	we (excludes listener)
	kita	we (includes listener)
	kamu	you (adult to child)
	mereka	they
	Pak	you (to an older/more important man)
	saya	I
	saudara	you (between adults of equal status)

Possessive adjectives		
	kami	our (excluding listener)
	kita	our (including listener)
	mereka	their
	saya	my
	saudara	your
	-nya	his/her (possessive suffix)

Verbs				
	beli	to buy	masak	to cook
	datang	to come	minum	to drink
	makan	to eat	sampai	to arrive
	mandi	to have a bath	tidur	to sleep

Tense markers				
	akan	will	kemarin	yesterday
	baru	recently, to have just	masih	still
			sedang	is . . . . . . ing
	belum	not yet	semalam	last night
	besok	tomorrow	sudah	already

Conjunction		Prepositions	
dan	and	di	at, in
		ke	to

Negative		Question marker	
tidak	no/not	apakah	(shows questions)

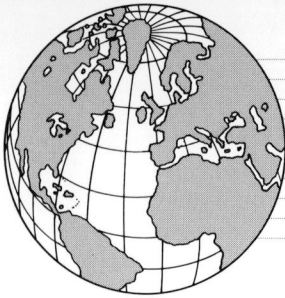

10 Language Spare Parts

As we have seen earlier, the English we use today owes much to Latin, which came into the language mainly at the time of the Norman invasion of Britain. In the following exercises we are going to explore the way the English language uses small, additional 'spare-parts' added to words to change their meaning and often their function — the way they work in a sentence. We have seen how language works through rules and patterns. These rules and patterns of a language are called its *grammar*.

A What do the following grammatical terms mean: *noun*; *adjective*; *verb*; *adverb*?

PREFIXES

We are going to look at some 'spare-parts' which are often added at the beginning of words. You will need to look for clues in both parts of the following short extracts from some conversations. Read them all through first.

Conversation 1
- The dodo was a strange bird. Did you know it's now extinct?
- I know. It died out about a hundred years ago.

Conversation 2
- Do you know I have just paid John £100 for this television and it doesn't work. I think that's extortionate.
- Go round and see him. He got all that money out of you for nothing.

Conversation 3
- On offer today! Fragrance of the month! Come and buy! Extract of roses.
- I'll get some for Auntie Maud. It says here that they've taken concentrated oil out of thousands of roses.

Conversation 4
- This is extraordinary! I can't believe my eyes, Dr. Watson.
- It is quite outside my ordinary experience too, Holmes.

126

Conversation 5

– Come along there! Arms stretch! Up, up up! Extend those arms to the ceiling.
– I'm really tired. I can't stretch my arms out another inch.

Notice that all the first speakers use a word starting with EX:
1 extinct **2** extortion **3** extract **4** extraordinary **5** extend.
The second speakers all use the word **out**.
EX is a word which comes from Latin and means 'out of' or 'from'.
All the Romance languages use such prefixes in the same way.

Read the following conversation:

Conversation 1

– You must come over and see grand-dad's collection of pre-war photographs.
– I'd love to. I've heard his photos go back to well before the 1920s.

Conversation 2

– This book has a very boring preface. Do I have to read it?
– Yes. It contains a lot of useful information which you are supposed to read before going onto the main text in the book.

Conversation 3

– The case is over and she's been found guilty. That judge was prejudiced against her from the start.
– Well that's bad. Judges are not supposed to judge anything before they've heard the evidence.

Conversation 4

– You know I had a premonition that something was wrong.
– You mean you knew before it happened? You must be psychic!

Notice that the first speaker uses **PRE** in the words:
1 pre-war **2** preface **3** prejudice **4** premonition.
The word used to match it by the second speaker is **before**.
PRE also comes from Latin, where it is written **prae** and means 'before' or 'in front of'.

We have seen how **EX** and **PRE** can be placed *in front of* some English words to extend, enlarge, modify and change the meaning of that word. Remember that these additions are called *prefixes*.

___

B Where does the word *prefix* come from? Break it down into two parts.
How can prefixes change the meaning of words? Here are some examples. Find some more of your own:

*ex*tend *dis*tend *pre*tend *por*tend.

___

Vocabulary Work

We can often break up a word into different parts and learn something about how it came to carry its present meaning. Look at the following example:

To Abduct

Prefix – **AB**
Meaning of prefix – *from/away*
Meaning of main word – *to lead*
Whole word – *to lead away*

Now do the same with the following words:
Use the Latin vocabulary list printed below.

1	aberration	**2**	to abjure
3	abnormal	**4**	to adapt
5	prefix	**6**	proclamation
7	to incarcerate	**8**	to induce
9	injection	**10**	to influence
11	to rebel	**12**	to reclaim.

Latin Vocabulary

AB	from/away
AD	to/towards
APTUS	fit
BELLUM	war
CARCER	a prison
CLAMO	I call
DUCO	I lead
ERRO	I wander
FIXUS	fixed
FLUERE	to flow
IN	in or into
JACIO	I throw
JURO	I swear or take an oath
PRO	in favour of
RE	again (or anew)

SUFFIXES

A *suffix* is another useful language part. The word comes from the Latin, **suffigere** meaning 'to fix under' and is made up of two parts, **sub**, meaning 'beneath, below or afterwards' (though here it has changed its final letter to F) and **figere** meaning 'to fix'.

A suffix is added at the end of a word to change the word's function. Suffixes allow us to make up new words on the same stem. English as a language is very good at this and this is one of the reasons why English has such a large vocabulary. Some common English suffixes are:

LY IVE TION FY
As in the words: lively
imaginative, imagination
satisfy, satisfaction

D Think of some more English words which contain any of these suffixes. What kind of words are they: nouns, adjectives, verbs, adverbs?

E **ISM** is a suffix which forms nouns expressing states or systems of ideas, i.e. principles. What do these words mean? Discuss your answers then write them down.

1 socialism
2 feminism
3 racism

What suffix would you use to turn these words into words meaning the person who holds those ideas?

ION (sometimes **SION, TION, XION,**) is usually added to make a noun from a verb.

e.g. | **Noun** | **Verb** |
|---|---|
| action | to act |
| decision | to decide |
| temptation | to tempt |

F Now find verbs for these nouns:

1 consideration
3 conclusion
2 presentation
4 concentration.

ABLE/IBLE this suffix makes adjectives from verbs and nouns.

e.g.: *suggestible* – She is a very suggestible person, i.e. she is very easy to persuade that stories or events are true.
manageable – This is quite manageable. I could do it easily.

G What do the following words mean? Look them up in a dictionary if necessary, then use each one in a sentence:

adjustable   capable   durable

H **ITY**. Add this suffix to adjectives in the last section and thereby change them all into nouns. Write the answers in your own books.

e.g.: suggestible – suggestibility
manageable – manageability
navigable   –
adjustable   –
capable   –
durable   –

We have looked at some common prefixes. We have also examined some common English suffixes.

Some languages also have a language part known as an *infix* which you will study in the unit on Language Invention.

I Invent an infix for 'small' and make up some imaginary words with it. Write their meaning beside them.

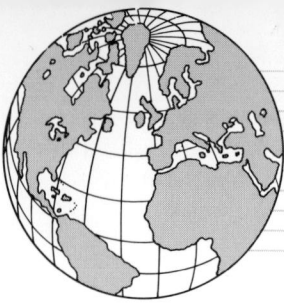

11 Language Invention

Invention is not unusual in languages. All languages need new *words* because the human race has been finding new objects, and inventing and producing new things and machines throughout its history. We can either call newly discovered things by the word for another object that is similar to them, or 'borrow' the word from another language, or use a Latin or Greek root to make a new word. Alternatively, we may invent words by putting words that already exist together, or use the name of the inventor.

A Below you will find a list of words which have entered the English language since the fifteenth century. Decide which kind of 'new' word each one is.

alligator	software
blitz	supersonic
chic	television
hoover	underpass
pineapple	wellington boots

Use an *etymological dictionary* to check if you were right.

As well as inventing new words we have also invented a number of 'new' languages which have been highly successful and are very widely used.

B Can you think of any? Look at the clues below and make a list of the languages used in each activity.

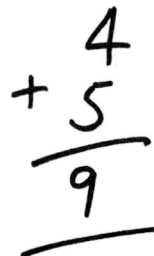

a

b

c

d

e

f

The languages illustrated here include some of the most recently invented ones. Can you find out when they were created? Can you use any or all of these languages? Have you ever tried making up a language with your friends so that your parents and teachers cannot understand what you are saying? If you have, describe how it works.

What do all these 'invented' languages have in common?

The 'languages' above are recent inventions. The languages spoken all round the world had been developing for thousands of years before the first of these was invented.

ESPERANTO

Some people believe it would be useful to have a universal language that everybody could speak and which could make communication easier between different peoples. Several 'artificial languages' have been invented, the most important of which is *Esperanto*.

Esperanto at a Glance

The Alphabet of Esperanto

A a	B b	C c	Ĉ ĉ	D d
ah	bo	tso	cho	do
E e	F f	G g	Ĝ ĝ	H h
eh	fo	go	Joe	ho
Ĥ ĥ	I i	J j	Ĵ ĵ	K k
hho	ee	yo	zho	ko
L l	M m	N n	O o	
lo	mo	no	oh	
P p	R r	S s	Ŝ ŝ	T t
po	ro	so	sho	toe
U u	Ŭ ŭ	V v	Z z	
oo	woe	vo	zo	

28 Letters. There is no Q, W, X, or Y.

A, E, I, O, U have approximately the vowel sounds heard in Are thEre thrEE Or twO.

C is not sounded like S or K, but like *ts* in *tsetse-fly*, *bits*.

J has the sound of *y* in *yes*.

The sounds of Ĉ, Ĝ, Ĥ, Ĵ, Ŝ, and Ŭ are heard in *leech*, *liege*, *loch*, *leisure*, *leash*, and *leeway*.

♪

ESPERANTO IS PHONETIC.

All letters sounded: one letter one sound.

ACCENT or STRESS falls on the last syllable but one.

NO IRREGULARITIES.   NO EXCEPTIONS.

THE GRAMMAR is based upon SIXTEEN FUNDAMENTAL RULES, which have no exceptions.

THE PARTS OF SPEECH are formed from Root-Words by the addition of appropriate Letters.

O is the ending for all names of things (NOUNS)

fakto	gluo
distanco	fajro
piano	tasko

ADJECTIVES (descriptive words) end in **A**

evidenta	freŝa
longa	furioza
granda	simpla

NOUNS and ADJECTIVES form PLURALS by adding **J**

evidentaj	longaj	grandaj
faktoj	distancoj	pianoj (*aj, oj* sound as in *my boy*)

THE SIMPLE VERB HAS ONLY SIX ENDINGS.

INFINITIVE	PRESENT	PAST	FUTURE	CONDITIONAL	IMPERATIVE
I	**AS**	**IS**	**OS**	**US**	**U**
ESTI	estas	estis	estos	estus	estu
LERNI	lernas	lernis	lernos	lernus	lernu
HELPI	helpas	helpis	helpos	helpus	helpu

N marks the ACCUSATIVE (*direct object*).

Mi (I) *helpas* lin (him)
Li (he) *helpas* min (me)
Ŝi lernas Esperanton

ADVERBS end in **E**

energie
entuziasme
diligente

131

Esperanto was devised by Dr Lazarus Ludwig Zamenhof from Warsaw in 1887. He intended Esperanto to be taught as everybody's second language so that it could be used as an *international language*, to make communication easier between peoples and countries.

Esperanto is easy to learn because it keeps to the rules Dr Zamenhof laid down; it is a very 'regular' language.

Of course, all languages have rules, but they also often break them. We only have to look at English to see how frequently this happens. For example:

Plurals

one horse		two horses
	but	
one sheep		two sheep
one mouse		two mice
one ox		two oxen

Past tense

talk		talk**ed**
	but	
speak		spoke
sing		sang
weep		wept

The student of English could also be forgiven for thinking there are no 'spelling rules' at all!

Because Esperanto is an invented language words can be made to keep to the rules. For example:

Nouns	All end in **o**	**libro**	book
		ŝtono	stone
		frato	brother
		fratino	sister
		koko	cock
		kokino	hen
		knabo	boy
		knabino	girl
Adjectives	All end in **a**	**bona**	good
		bela	beautiful
		granda	large
		varma	warm
Plurals	Suffix **j**	**fratoj**	brothers
Articles	No indefinite 'a'; 'the' is always **la**	**la frato**	the brother
		la fratoj	the brothers
Verbs	Infinitives all end in **i**	**havi**	to have
		ludi	to play
		esti	to be
		vidi	to see

Verbs (cont.)	All verbs end in **s** Present: Past: Future:	**mi havas** I have **ŝi havas** she has **mi havis** I had **mi havos** I will have
Adverbs	All end in **e**	**varme** warmly

It is very easy to form words from others because the endings tell you what *part of speech* each word is.

C   What do these words mean? Write the answers in your exercise books.

viv*o* = life   **viv*as***
viv*a*   **viv*is***
viv*e*   **viv*os***

The Esperanto for 'love' is **ami**. How would you say the following?
1 loving   **2** lovingly   **3** will love   **4** loved   **5** loves.

The Esperanto Alphabet

Dr Zamenhof created an alphabet of twenty-eight letters. This was made up of twenty-two Roman letters, plus:

ĵ   (as in jour Fr.)   **ĵunalo**   a newspaper
ŭ   to show a *diphthong*   **ankaŭ**   also
                      (where two vowels
                      run together)
Try and guess the remaining four.

D   What sounds do the Esperanto letters ĉ, ĝ, ĵ and ŝ make? Look at the words below and sound them out.

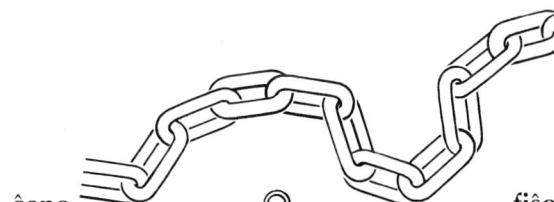

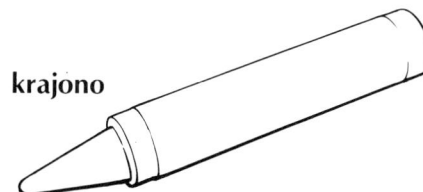

ĉeno   fiŝo

kaĝo   krajono

Every word is spelt exactly as it sounds in Esperanto. There are no silent letters. The 'stress' is always on the next to last syllable.

In Unit Ten, Language Spare Parts, we found out a lot about prefixes and suffixes and spoke about a 'spare part' that is not used in

English: the *infix*. Esperanto uses all these spare parts and has several important *infixes* that are very useful in building up a large vocabulary. For example:

-ar- shows a collection
  arbo = tree   **arb*ar*o** = wood

-er- shows a part of the whole
  ĉeno = a link from a chain   **ĉen*er*o** = a chain

-eg- shows intensity or augments
  pluvo = rain   **pluv*eg*o** = a downpour

-et- is a diminutive
  domo = house   **dom*et*o** = cottage

E 1 What does the infix **-in-** show? Refer back to the noun section on the previous page. Use all the infixes you already know to help you.
   2 How would you say the following?
     a drizzle   **b** chick
     c mansion   **d** library
     e little girl   **f** boulder
     g pebble

As Esperanto is based on the Romance languages, English, German and Russian it is quite easy for speakers of European languages to master.

F Can you work out the following sentences? Most of the words you already know but you will have to guess a few.

1 **La fiŝo estas freŝa.**
2 **La du libroj estas en la dometo.**
3 **Mi havas granda domo en la bela arbaro.**
4 **Tri birdoj en unu kaĝo.**
5 **La kokino kaj la koketoj vivis en arboj en la granda arbaro.**
6 **En arbaro estas multaj belaj floroj kaj grandaj arboj.**

Now write the following sentences in Esperanto.

1 The warm drizzle.
2 The little girls are in the cottage.
3 I have three big books in the library.
4 The two sisters are playing in the house.
5 She saw a cock, a hen and some chicks on the rocks.
6 A boy is playing in the library.

Today there are about eight million speakers of Esperanto around the world. Many books have been translated and published in the language including a number of technical dictionaries. There are at least 110 periodicals in Esperanto appearing regularly.

However we need to recognise that although speakers of Esperanto do come from all over the world and it has achieved some success as an international language, no more speak Esperanto than do, for example, Swedish or Bulgarian. Even Jonkha, the national language

of a tiny country like Bhutan in Southern Asia has one million speakers. So, in spite of the advantages of Esperanto, it still has some way to go before it can be recognized as a 'universal language'.

G Can you list the advantages and disadvantages of Esperanto as a world language. Here are some suggestions.

It is regular and easy to learn.
It could be everybody's second language.
It has no historic or political overtones, so would be neutral when used in negotiations or disputes.

It is based mainly on European languages.
It has no literary tradition.
It is nobody's first language.

Do the lists you have made tell us anything about the way people feel about languages and in particular about their own mother tongue or first language?

We can see very clearly just from the few rules and vocabulary we have looked at in Esperanto, how it works and what a regular language it is. By inventing a language together we can gain some insight into how the languages we already know function because we have to think about the grammar and structures that we are creating. It should also show us that to understand and convey meaning accurately we often have to look at the details very carefully since, unfortunately, neither English nor the languages which you learn at school are completely 'regular'. We still have to learn their rules and know what the exceptions are.

INVENTING A LANGUAGE

Let us call our language WiLoP.

Alphabet and Punctuation

The most important decision is whether we are going to invent a completely new alphabet or use one which already exists. You are familiar with a number of scripts now, but since there would be little point in us creating anything but the most straightforward of languages we have decided to use the *Roman script*. However, as there are two different sounds to the letter 's', we can follow the German rule and use ß for a 'ss' sound.

Punctuation will be as for English yet retaining the useful ¿ or inverted question mark at the beginning of sentences as used in Spanish. **¿Cómo te llamas?** What is your name?

```
a b c d e f g h i j k l m n o p q r s t
u v w x y z ß
,  ;  .  :  !  !  ?  ¿  . . .   "  "
```

Nouns and Articles

Our first decision here is whether we are going to have noun 'genders' for objects. Of course, people and animals will still be masculine and feminine. English has no gender for objects. Spanish and French have masculine and feminine and German has three genders: masculine, feminine and neuter.

They all use definite articles i.e. 'the', in English. Spanish has **el**, **la**, **los** and **las**; French has **le**, **la** and **les**; and German has **der**, **die**, **das** and **die**, when used with a subject. We will opt for the simplest, and keep to one definite article and no gender for objects. We will, however, show whether our nouns are 'living' or not:
i.e.   **paßot**   passport
      baßet   dog
Our article will be **ha** used as a prefix as in Hebrew.
Many languages, among them Bahasa Indonesia and Chinese, do not use the indefinite article so we can omit any word for 'a'.
Noun plurals will be formed by adding the suffix **-ra** which is one way of forming plurals in Bengali.

Nouns and articles	
paßot	(a) passport
hapaßot	the passport
hapaßotra	the passports

Adjectives

Adjectives precede the noun in English and German. They normally follow the noun in French, Spanish and Arabic. In languages with genders they normally make some change to show the gender.

e.g.   *le* **couteau vert**   the green knife
        la **maison vert*e***   the green house
        les **maison*s* vert*es***   the green houses

As we have already decided to have no genders in WiLoP, we only have to decide if we want them to agree with plural nouns. Let us opt for adjectives to end in **-i** and to follow the noun. Plurals will be formed in the same way as plurals of nouns.

Adjectives:
spanioli	Spanish
paßot spanioli	a Spanish passport
paßot*ra* spanioli*ra*	some Spanish passports

Adverbs

In English adverbs are formed by adding 'ly' to adjectives.

e.g. 'Lucky' thus becomes 'luckily'. In French, German and Spanish there are alternative ways of making adverbs. You can use the *noun* and make an adverb by putting 'with' before it; i.e. 'with luck' means the same as 'luckily'. You can also take the *feminine adjective* and add **-ment** (French) or **-mente** (Spanish). Alternatively, the adverb may be identical to the adjective, as in German.

e.g. **schnell** means 'quick' or 'quickly'. Here we will opt for showing the adverb by writing it with a capital letter and adding **-ly** as in English.

Adverbs
rapidi	quick
Rapidily	quickly

Verbs

The languages of the world have very many different ways of dealing with the complexities of the verb. Some, like Bahasa Indonesia, never change but use tense markers. At the other end of the scale some, like Spanish, change for almost every person. Many languages show 'tenses' so in WiLoP we will continue to have endings to show past, present and future with the prefix **le** to indicate the 'infinitive'; e.g. *le*mandu, meaning 'to send'. The verb 'to be' will be omitted at all times.

e.g. **Habaßet grandi**   The dog (is) big

In order to be clear who is doing the action, our simple verbs will need 'pronouns'. If we are sure to keep to a clear word order we can use our pronouns for 'subject' and 'object' and even as 'possessive adjectives' as well, as in Bahasa Indonesia.

Pronouns and possessive adjectives	
saya	I, me, my
tu	you, your (sing, familiar form)
Viptu	you, your (sing, formal form)
er	he, him, his
sie	she, her
we	we, us, our
vos	you, your (plural, familiar form)
Vipvos	you, your (plural, formal form)
hem	they, them, theirs (masculine)
hen	they, them, theirs (feminine)

Verbs	
*le*mandu	*to* send
mandu	send, sending (present)
mandao	sent (past)
mandil	*will* send (future)

e.g. **Saya mandao hapaßot.**
I sent the passport.
¿Vipvos mandil hapaßotra dashira?
Will you (form. plural) send the new passports?

Nuts and Bolts

Prepositions to = **ke** from = **min** in = **dans**

Conjunctions with = **con** and = **plus** but = **aber**

Negatives neg . . . . neg on either side of verb
negneg in case of omission of 'to be'

Interrogatives Questions are formed by inserting ¿ . . . . ? with no other change necessary.
Ubi = where? **Quand** = when?

Vocabulary

Nouns

ganot	park	**baßet**	dog
paßot	passport	**solmet**	friend
bilot	ticket	**blumet**	plant
meßagot	letter	**ayamet/ayamot**	chicken
oficialot	town-hall		

Adjectives

spanioli	Spanish	**baiki**	good/nice
großi	big	**baiki prixot**	cheap
picoli	little	**rapidi**	quick
leati	slow	**dashi**	new

Adverbs	**Rapidily**	quickly	**Baikily prixot**	cheaply
	Leatily	slowly	**Baikily**	well

Verbs	**lemandu**	to send	**letravelu**	to go
	leknotu	to buy	**legernu**	to want
	levidelu	to see	**lescriptu**	to write
	lemangu	to eat	**lepasmatu**	to come in
	lemanu	to get/receive		

Write the English for the following WiLoP sentences:

1 **Saya travelu ke haoficialot con hameßagot.**
2 **Jeremy mangu ayamot picoli.**
3 **¿Bilotra con hapaßot?**
4 **Sie videlao blumetra großira dans hagamot.**
5 **Saya gernu lescriptu meßagot ke haprofeßetra Rapidily.**
6 **¿Quand tu knotil habilotra?**
7 **Hen travelao con habaßet ke hagamot baiki.**
8 **Tu neg mandu neg bilotra ke tu solmet spanioli aber ke saya.**
9 **Hem knotao ayametra großira Baikily prixot.**
10 **¿Ubi Vipvos pasmatu oficialot?**

Can you write these sentences in WiLoP?

1 The dog is in the park.
2 I want to see the letters quickly.
3 Is he well?
4 Where do I buy tickets cheaply?
5 We received the passport with a letter from the town-hall.
6 Our friend in Spain does not write long letters to us.
7 He eats slowly. He is not well.
8 When and where did you see the cheap plants?
9 He wants to receive letters but he doesn't want to write to you.
10 I don't want to write WiLoP. It's no good.

Try making up your own language with completely different rules. Use the 'parts of speech' list that we used to make up WiLoP, so that you do not forget to think about the way sentences function. You could try using the same vocabulary at least to start with, though you might want to add some more words later.

Inventonu happioni!   Happy Inventing!

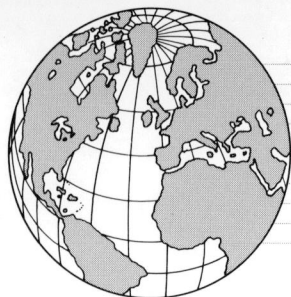

Did you know?

1 . . . that by 1965, the Bible Society had translated the Scriptures into over 1200 languages?

2 . . . that the two most highly populated cities in the world are Spanish and Portuguese speaking (Mexico City and São Paulo, with 13 and 12.75 millions respectively).

3 . . . that Nigeria in 1986, was the eighth most populous country in the world but by the year 2001, it is estimated that it will hold third place with a population of 509 million? India will be first, followed by China.

4 . . . that in Anglo-Saxon nouns were masculine, feminine or neutral? (Gender definitions which German has retained).

5 . . . that Somalia is the only country in Africa whose inhabitants all speak one language as a mother tongue? (Somali).

6 . . . that the word 'shuttle', which we now use in the context of space travel, meant originally, in the eighteenth century, a fast moving wooden component of mill looms?

7 . . . that the letters in the Hebrew alphabet each have a numerical value?

8 . . . that all words beginning with auto-, hetero-, hydr-, phon-, meta- and hyper- and ending in -ology and -ism, come from Greek?

9 . . . that Lardie Moonlight who died in the early 1980s was the last speaker of the Australian Aboriginal language, Kalkadoon?

10 . . . that the words 'aerial', 'bump' and 'dwindle' appeared for the first time in the works of Shakespeare?

11 . . . that in English, 'casserole' denotes a method of cooking but in French it is just a cooking utensil?

12 . . . that it was only discovered at the end of the eighteenth century that Sanskrit showed affinities with Latin, Greek and other European languages? (Hence the term 'Indo-European' family of languages.)

13 . . . that the country of Upper Volta changed its name to Burkino Faso, which means 'land of upright people?'

14 . . . that the Republic of Cameroon in Africa has two official languages, English and French?

15 . . . that the country of Lichtenstein has a population of 38,000, its currency is the Swiss Franc, it is smaller than Washington DC and its language is German? (Alemannisch dialect.)

16 . . . that Cajun, a form of Old French, is spoken in parts of Louisiana?

17 . . . that the six official languages of the United Nations are Arabic, Chinese, English, French, Russian and Spanish?

18 . . . that Andorra has been run jointly by France and the Bishops of Urgel since 1278 and its official language is Catalan?

19 . . . that KYPRIAKI DIMOKRATIA and KIBRIS CUMHURIYE are the respective Greek and Turkish names of Cyprus?

20 . . . that in India Assamese, Bengali, Gujarati, Hindi, Kannada, Kannarese, Kashmiri, Malayalam, Marathi, Oriya, Panjabi, Sindhi, Tamil, Telugu, Urdu are the official languages recognised by the Constitution?

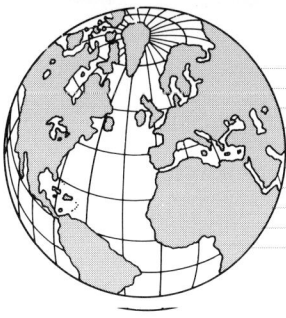

Index